THE KINGDOM

GOLD EDITION

Teacher's Manual

By Ginny Seymour

Cover Illustrator
Tammy C Dickson

Evensong Publishing

THE KINGDOM TEACHER'S MANUAL- Gold Edition
Copyright @ 1999
All Rights reserved
Printed in the United States of America
Library of Congress TX 5-633-879
ISBN 0-9718325-3-6

No part of this workbook may be used or reproduced in any manner whatsoever without the express written permission of the publisher except in a brief quotation in a review. *The Kingdom Teacher's Manual* also contains a complete copy of *The Kingdom,* ISBN 0-978325-0-1, Copyright TX 5-633-879. All scriptures are from the Holy Bible, New International Version, copyright 1973, 1978, 1984 International Bible Society and are used with the permission of Zondervan Bible Publishers.

Table of Contents

THE KINGDOM TEACHER'S MANUAL - GOLD EDITION
13 Prophetic Actions

A Word from the Author

	Introduction	1 ™
CHAPTER ONE	**RESTORATION OF THE KINGDOM**	
Session One	Thy Kingdom Come	3 ™
Session Two	Patterns of the Kingdom - Patterns of the World	4 ™
CHAPTER TWO	**THE EVERLASTING KINGDOM**	
Session One	The Triune God	7 ™
Session Two	The Statement of Belief	8 ™
CHAPTER THREE	**TTHE TRUE AND FAITHFUL KING**	
Session One	The King's Invitation	9 ™
Session Two	The Word of God	10 ™
Session Three	The Contract Signed in Blood	11 ™
CHAPTER FOUR	**PREPARE FOR THE KINGDOM**	
Session One	Repentance and Holiness	12 ™
Session Two	Be Baptized with Water and the Spirit	13 ™
CHAPTER FIVE	**THE KINGDOM STANDARDS**	
Session One	Love - The Law of the Kingdom	14 ™
Session Two	Forgiveness - an Act of Love	15 ™
Session Three	Faith - Kingdom Principles	17 ™
Session Four	Hope - The Promise of the Kingdom	18 ™
CHAPTER SIX	**THE KINGDOM HEALTH PLAN**	
Session One	Healing - The Song of the Kingdom	20 ™
Session Two	The Commission	21 ™

SUPPLEMENTARY MATERIALS

Supplementary Supply List		22 ™
Chapter 1	The Names of God, Scribe Page	23 ™
Chapter 2	The Apostles' Creed	26 ™
Chapter 3	The King's Invitation, The Play, Worksheet	27 - 32 ™
Chapter 4	The Four Gospels	33 - 36 ™
Chapter 5	Love is a Choice, The Law of Love, Love never Fails	37 - 39 ™
	The Kingdom Map	40 - 41 ™

THE COMPLETE TEXT OF THE KINGDOM .... 1 - 76

13 Prophetic Actions

"Prepare the way for the Lord!
Make straight in the wilderness
a highway for our God."
Isaiah 40:3

WRESTLING WITH GOD	5TM
MUSTARD SEED FAITH	5TM
THE SHOUT OF HOLY	10TM
THE CUP OF FRIENDSHIP	11TM
STRIKE THE GROUND	15TM
HEALING THE HEART	16TM
SPEAK TO CIRCUMSTANCES	17TM
THE DEPOSIT OF FAITH	18TM
THE WALK OF SIGNS AND WONDERS	18TM
THE HONOR CHAIR	19TM
THE BLESSING	21TM
THE GREAT COMMISSION	21TM
THE FOOT WASHING CEREMONY	21TM

Word from the Author

Behold The Kingdom

Welcome teachers to *The Kingdom Teacher's Manual*. This manual is structured as a tool to impart the basic truths of Christian living. It is a book of Kingdom wisdom and a book of Kingdom prayers. It has been prepared with great diligence and attention to detail to supplement the text *The Kingdom - Christian Primary I*. The text *The Revolution Begins* is a journal that has been prepared as a workbook to accompany *The Kingdom* when taught as a Bible study.

This text teaches concepts that forshadow living in continious relationship with God: a base understanding of how God speaks as a triune God, how to perform prophetic actions that bring forth supernatural results, how to hear God speak . These practices have application far beyond this study. This study reaches inside you to pull forth the God relationship you destined to live.

This is a very compressed overview of Kingdom living and it emcompasses enormous territory. Other Christians have written volumes covered here maybe in a sentence or two. Learning and applying all this information takes time and the guidance of the Holy Spirit.

This text represents my journey to know God. It is the first in a three-part *Christian Primary* series...primary meaning the simplest or most basic information one needs to know. *The Glory - Christian Primary II* teaches man and his anointing, along with the meaning of color and numbers. *The Power - Christian Primary III* imparts the gifts and fruits of the Holy Spirit and deliverance. All work is derived from my own research unless otherwise notated.

I dedicate *The Kingdom Teacher's Manual* to my family. I wish to thank all those who prayed and encouraged me along the way, especially Tammy Dickson for her faithful assistance in developing the artwork and Reverend John Sandford for introducing to me the concept of Inner Healing.

I pray for you, the teacher of these materials: *May the eyes of your heart be enlightened in order that you may know the hope to which He has called you, the riches of His glorious inheritance in the saints, and His (God's) incomparably great power for us who believe (Ephesians 1:18-19).*

I have been in bondage and now am free. I have found these treasures of the Kingdom. Into your hands I pour these treasures.

For the Kingdom,

Ginny

INTRODUCTION
THE KINGDOM TEACHER'S MANUAL
Changing the World one Heart at a Time

In the Great Commission Jesus directs His followers, "*Go therefore and make disciples of all nations, baptizing them in the name of the Father and of the Son and of the Holy Spirit and teaching them to obey everything I have commanded you (Matthew 28: 18-20).*" The Kingdom Teacher's Manual imparts the power of Kingdom living. It is a book of Kingdom wisdom and a book of Kingdom prayers.

The goal of this Kingdom material is to teach the trinue language of God and to map a blueprint to set God's people free. Each lesson offers the opportunity for all to be actively involved. The lessons throughout The Kingdom Teacher's Manual are structured so participants apply the knowledge they acquire as application is the highest level of learning. The objectives of the lessons are: to offer a sound overview, to bring balance in teaching and to build a Kingdom foundation for believers. The target audience of this teaching is those who will commit to become true disciples (intimate friends) with Jesus.

The Kingdom explores the triune nature of God and teaches His triune language. God is Father, Son and Holy Spirit. God created man: body, soul and spirit. The standards of the Kingdom living are three: hope, faith and love. Here this Kingdom pattern is purposely placed in order to impart Kingdom understanding. Areas teaching the triune Kingdom pattern are clearly marked by a triangle.

The Kingdom study uses art, music and drama to convey Kingdom understanding. These materials present an orderly and solid overview of God's eternal Kingdom: doctrine, truths, principles, prayers and practices. This study on God's Kingdom is simply soaked in Scripture, incorporating over 500 Scripture references in The Kingdom and The Kingdom Teacher's Manual, a thorough read-through of all of the New Testament and includes individual, encouraging Scriptures.

Chapters are divided into sessions. Begin each session with prayer, a couple of songs and a brief, but limited sharing time. Do not allow one person to dominate! Always allow discussion as discussion helps internalize understanding. Suggested ways to teach each session and a supplementary material list has been included. Supplementary pages, except for the Kingdom map, are on the same page numbers in The Kingdom Teacher's Manual (Teacher's handbook) as they are in the student's Journal - The Revolution Begins. Direct teaching instructions are in Talking Point or the Wrap, and are contained in quotes.

Always have each person draw a Scripture from the Scripture Box at the end of each session. How God personally speaks to them is then recorded in the Kingdom Journal and shared. Scriptures have not been assigned for a most important reason. It is here we come to God as an individual and let God speak to us. Our personal relationship with God is not to be controlled by another. God chooses the Scripture to speak to the heart of each individual through the Scripture drawn from a box of Scriptures. End each lesson with a Kingdom parable. Close with the Lord's Prayer and/or spontaneous prayer.

Prophetic actions throughout this text move the participant into entering into the supernatural Kingdom on a level perhaps new to them. Expect full participation.

Savor the 13+ Kingdom prayers, 13 prophetic actions, the three Kingdom quests, the play, the choral reading, the shout of holy, the map of the Kingdom, the Law of Love! View the historical document - *The Apostles' Creed*, enjoy original gospel art from the ancient *Book of Kells* and learn to speak the triune language of God.

Encourage and pray for participants. Stretch yourself and attempt new approaches to teaching recommended in the lessons. And most importantly, allow the Holy Spirit to be your guide and inspiration as you adapt this Kingdom project to your needs.

All Rights are Copyright Protected

Master sheets are included in *The Kingdom Teacher's Manual* for the teacher's use only. *The Revolution Begins - The Kingdom Journal* is for the student. These books are covered under copyright law and there are no rights of reproduction. All rights are the sole ownership of Evensong Publishing.

The prints of the four gospels from, *The Book of Kells* is printed with permission from CELTIC DESIGN Coloring Book by Ed Sibbet Jr. Copyright by Dover Publications, Inc. 31 East 2nd Street, Mineola, NY, 11501. Prints have been included in your packet for you to color and use as a pictorial demonstration of the power of the Gospels. You can also obtain the coloring book by contacting Dover Publications at the above address.

The Kingdom map, and most supplementary pages, are also found in the Kingdom Journal -*The Revolution Begins*, with the exception of, *The Apostles' Creed,* and the names of God. These pages are only in *The Kingdom Teacher's Manual*. Custom pictures from *The Book of Kells* and interior art, including the Kingdom map, are courtesy of Tammy Dickson. *The Revolution Begins i*s the Kingdom Journal for participants that allows opportunities to record prayers, Scripture readings and text assignments.

Supplementary Materials List
Book: *The Name Book* by Dorothea Austin
Music*:* Music by Michael W. Smith. Use with the play -*The Wise Little King,* and at the Cup of Friendship. Other praise and worship music as befitting the age group attending.
Other: Name tags, several boxes of colored pencils, anointing oil, a box of Scripture quotes, a Cross, whiteboard, dry erase pens (for the teacher) and crowns for the play.

OPTIONAL MATERIALS - To check out or to Incorporate in class.
Books: *Power in Praise* by Merlin Carothers - suggested supplementary text
Tape: *The Story of the Highest Bidder,* by Ginny Seymour can be purchased as additional material to be used with chapter three with session two or three
Suggested Movies: *The Passion of the Christ* by Mel Gibson, *The Ten Commandments* by Cecil De Mill and *The Prince of Egypt* by Dreamworks.

*The Book of Kells is the richest, most pictorial, and colorful, early version of the four Gospels. Decorated in the Celto-Saxon style art by early Christians, it is attributed to St. Columba and the Abbey of Kells. Currently, *The Book of Kells,* can be found in the library at Trinity College in Dublin, Ireland. This text dates between 600 to 800 and is considered an Irish, national treasure.

Chapter One RESTORATION OF THE KINGDOM

The Kingdom
The supernatural realm where,
God, Creator of all of the Universe,
Reigns supreme.

SESSION ONE

Theme: Thy Kingdom Come
Activities: Getting to Know Each Other - Beginning the Journey
Resources: A Word from The Author, The Scribe's Page, The Scripture Page, Robert Frost Poem - The Road Not Taken, Whiteboard

<u>Introduction:</u> Greet one another. Say a prayer, sing a song, have a cookie, juice and/or tea. Take time for introductions. Who are the people who came? What roads did they take to get here? Why have they come? Preview the table of contents and a word from the author, in their Kingom journals *The Revolution Begins*.

Enter their names in their Kingdom journal *The Revolution Begins*. Read the footnote from the Prophet Jeremiah. Read aloud and discuss the introduction to *Kingdom Dreams, Visions and Blueprints*.

The first sixteen pages in *The Revolution Begins,* are for notating the Scriptures God personally speaks. God chooses the Scripture as students drawn out of a Scripture box. Each of these pages allows space for contemplation on the meaning of what God is personally speaking to them. God desires a personal relationship with each of us.

Pages 17- 40 in *The Revolution Begins,* are pages to record prayers, prophetic actions, quests and pages to learn the names of God and the language of God. They also include the play, *The Wise Little King*, a salvation invitation, Gospel art, worksheets, the choral reading on love, places to record healing and a map of God's Kingdom.

Point out the Scribe Page on page 25. It is for each person to keep a weekly running log of observations of <u>positive attributes</u> for each person attending. Divide into groups of six if entire group is too large. Remind everyone at the end of each lesson to write down these <u>positive</u> notes. These notes will be used in chapter five.

Discussion: The Y in the Road Obtain a copy of Robert Frost's poem *The Road Not Taken* (at your public library or online). Frost chose the road less traveled and that has made all the difference! 1. Why did it make a difference? 2. How does the road one chooses determine their destination? 3.How do you think the road you choose will forever influence your destiny? So, if we must choose, let it be said of us, we have chosen wisely!

Talking Point: The Crossroad Draw picture of a Y on a whiteboard. "There is a crossroads, a literal, Y, in the road that lays before those who have chosen to take this Kingdom journey. It is a life-long journey to know and live in fellowship with God.

Choosing this road will make all the difference in your life! This day, all stand on the edge of a decision. Which road will they take? Knowing you are literally choosing to place your feet upon a path helps you understand the journey." (Share a brief testimony...how you came to this road.)

"Notice how closely the roads on the Y are together at the beginning of the journey, but soon how wide apart they become. Both roads look about the same. Be aware that to walk closer to God is a choice. During your lifetime, even if right now you choose the Kingdom crossroads, inside the Kingdom journey there will be other crossroads. There will be roads where you will have to choose the less traveled path for you to reach your destiny. God has a personal destiny for each one. Know when you stand at a crossroad. Choose the road that leads to Yahweh! Choose to be people that walk in God's way."

"Noah was a man who stood at a crossroads. God said to build an ark! When God called Noah to build a boat, Noah was not a ship builder. Noah built the ark and rode above the waters. As Noah rode above the waters he was a humble ship builder. But when Noah landed, he owned the whole world. This is your journey to know how to hear God's voice and build your boat so that you, too, may enter into God - appointed destiny."

"You can choose to be a part of God's everlasting Kingdom, where Jesus reigns as King. Come partake in the God's Kingdom (John 12:46)!"

WRAP: Read Jeremiah 6:16
READ: The Parable of the Great Banquet Luke 14:15-24
ASSIGNMENT: Draw from the Scripture Box. Allow time to copy Scripture in their Journal *The Revolution Begins* starting on page 3. Assign chapter one, *The Kingdom*.
Begin study in the Bible - Genesis chapters 1-35. Read five chapters daily.
CLOSE: The Lord's Prayer Page 14, *The Kingdom*

SESSION TWO The Kingdom pages 1-6, Kingdom TM 23-24, Kingdom Journal 23-24

Theme: Patterns of the Kingdom - Patterns of the World
Activities: Name Book and Names of God
Resources: *The Name Book* by Dorothea Austin, Whiteboard, Wrapped Package, Packet of Seeds, Scotch Tape

<u>Introduction:</u> This is the day for choosing the road you will take. Share the story of the *Pearl of Great Price* - the man gave all he had for this great treasure (Matthew 12:44). Review story of *The Great Banquet*. Some were too busy to come so the lord of the house sent into the highways and byways to invite anyone who will to come (Matthew 22: 1-10). So it is with us. We must decide. The table is set! The banquet is prepared! Ask any of them to share if they received a dream, vision or word from God. Reinforce that it It is better to write one word from God than millions of the world's words or thousands of their own words.

Share what they wrote in their Journals. Did God speak? What is God saying? Read together pages 1-3 in *The Kingdom*.

Talking Points: Patterns "There are two kinds of patterns - those of the world and, those of God's Kingdom. Godly patterns, truths and principles are constant and unchanging. Worldly patterns constantly shift. For teens, one pattern to be discussed is peer pressure. For adults, the pattern is often the fear of man. It's all about what other people think or how we've been taught. In God's Kingdom, what is important is what God thinks. We choose to be God pleasers! It is a choice. It is God's Kingdom path - God's Kingdom pattern." Read together Jeremiah 6:16 on page 4. Continue through page 6.

First Prophetic Action: Wrestling with God Use the following Scripture: *From the days of John the Baptist until now, the Kingdom of Heaven had been forcefully advancing and forceful men lay hold of it (Matthew 11:12).* Record prophetic action page 22, *The Revolution Begins.*

Everyone must contend with God to obtain His Kingdom. Have one person play the part of God - they will have the package you wrapped. Explain God has a destiny for each of us, but we have to wrestle with God for this gift if we really want it. Each person will have to go into the next room and wrestle with God for their package. (No real wrestling, just make them struggle to get the package. Each person who struggles always wins the package.) While each person is wrestling for their package, the others are the great cloud of witnesses. When the winner returns they cheer for them.

Second Prophetic Action: Mustard Seed Faith If someone would come and scatter hundred dollar bills on the floor everyone would scramble to get them. Today, pretend to be the Sower going forth to sow the Word of God. As you sow this seed in faith, so they can have faith if they grab hold of it. Have everyone get ready to grab their seed of faith. Scatter the seeds. Each one should find at least one tiny seed (Matthew 13:31-32). Then tell them the story of the mustard seed. The mustard seed from Israel is the smallest seed of all. If their faith is just that size they can move mountains. The mustard plant in Israel, grows to a height of 10 feet. Ten means ownership of the world. Use scotch tape and tape their seed in *The Revolution Begins*, page 22, under prophetic actions. This is all the faith they need. Recognize in all Kingdom things you don't even have to come up with your own seed! God supplies the seed you need for everything (2 Corinthians 9:10)!

Talking Point: It's all in a Name Look up the meanings of each person's name in, *The Name Book,* by Dorothea Austin. Share what their names mean and then write the meaning of their names, along with their name, in the beginning of *The Revolution Begins.* "God has called you to become His and inherit His Kingdom before you were ever formed in your mother's womb. God has already given you a clue to who you are. In the Jewish tradition, a person became his name. Your name has meaning. It is God who named you."

"Your name reinforces your destiny. Before the foundation of the world, God knew you and called you by name. He created you in His very image. He has numbered every hair on your head. He has carved them on the palm of His hands. If you were not precious, He would not have sacrificed His only Son to deliver you!"

Teaching: Who is God? Participants have been introduced and shared the meaning of their name. Now introduce God.

△ **Triune Language of God** God is one God, triune in nature. On the whiteboard make a medium - sized triangle. Place the word, God, in the middle of the triangle. On the top point place the name, God the Father. On the left corner write the name of Jesus, and on the right corner the name of the Holy Spirit. It is extremely important that you always follow these directions of the triangle diagram exactly every time you repeat the triune, language lesson.

As you study God and His triune nature, you will also be studying God's triune language. The triangle will be used four times in the study to reinforce God's triune nature and His triune language. All triangles can be superimosed over top of each other.

Talking Point: The Name of God "We have been focusing on the triune nature of God. Now we will more closely inspect and consider each area of the Godhead."

"God is triune and each part of the triune God has a name and, that name has meaning. As the lesson began, we found the meaning of each other's names and extended our understanding of who we are called to be. As we learned each other's names and meanings of those names our understanding was enlarged. So it is that to know God's name and call Him by His name enlarges our understanding of God."

"Find page 23 in your Kingdom Journal. Write in the first circle, God the Father." Ask for suggestions of names for God the Father. As names are brainstormed, start with the circle and draw a line away from the circle. Write a name on this line. Continue to add lines all around the circle. (When there are no more suggestions, share names from the Names of God in *The Kingdom Teacher's Manual,* page 23 -24. Repeat the lesson for the names of God the Son and the names of God the Holy Spirit.)

WRAP: "God is calling you forth to be the person He made you to be. He wants you to know Him and walk in His way. This is who God is: (point towards names) the mighty God of Creation, who offers you His love and His friendship. In His Kingdom you will be made rich in every way so that you can be generous on every occassion (Corinthians 9:10-11). He is a God who lives up to the meaning of His name."

ASSIGNMENT: God has chosen each of us to become His child. Who is this God? The following is a study of your God. Remind class to write on their Scribe Page. Read On. pages 7 -10 in *The Kingdom*. <u>Bible - Genesis 35-50 to Exodus 20:26.</u> Read five chapters a day. Record assignments in their Kingdom Journals. Scripture Box

READ: The Parable of the Mustard Seed Read Matthew 13:31-32 (and footnotes).
The Parable of the Sower Matthew 13:1-9, 18-23

CLOSE: The Lord's Prayer Lay hands on each heart. Pray that the seed of faith they receive will multiply a hundred fold. And, that those who receive this seed, become a Sower of seeds themselves, for it is to the Sower that seed is supplied.

Chapter Two — THE EVERLASTING KINGDOM

SESSION ONE   The Kingdom pages 7-10, Kingdom Journal page 26

Theme: The Triune God
Activity: Writing the Statement of Belief - The Believer's Manifesto

Introduction: The Statement of Belief Class will be formulating a Statement of Faith to establish the perimeters of the Kingdom of God using the Scriptures provided. Allow time to work through the lesson until everyone is completely satisfied. Open with prayer and praise. Review pages 7-10 in *The Kingdom.*

Checkpoint: Are they writing on their Scribe Page? Give them examples of positive actions you have observed. Remind them to write in this page after each session. If they are not writing in their Scriptures they can scotch tape them in their Kingdom Journals.

Talking Point: Triune God "God is triune, yet, He is one. How can that be? It is something we cannot understand with our human minds. God is who He says He is. He created man in His own image and man is a triune being: body, soul and spirit. Yet, we are one. He created the universe with the atom - the building block of all that exists. The atom contains three elements: protons, electrons and neutrons and yet it is just one. God created time in three sections: past, present and future. He created three heavens: the heaven above the earth, the heavens with the stars and the heaven where He sits upon His throne. He created color as coming from one light source, three colors that cannot be produced from other colors: yellow, red and blue. He is triune God creating in trinity."

Talking Point: The Believer's Manifesto "God is calling you as a follower of the Kingdom, as people who will faithfully live the Kingdom of God. You have chosen this way, this path, this journey. As Kingdom people, write a Statement of Belief to secure this path for yourselves and for future generations."

Small Group Activity: The Manifesto Divide into three groups. Each study group is to write a Statement of Belief, a document or declaration using the notes from the Scriptures on page 7-10 on their assigned name of God. Each group will compile their information and then condense it into three or four sentences stating the core issue of their study.

Allow thirty to forty minutes to draft statements. Suggest one person in each group act as a scribe. Check to see how the groups are progressing. If some finish sooner, use this time for a coffee and cookie break. Once everyone is finished, gather together and share conclusions. Compile information and copy in *The Revolution Begins*, page 26.

WRAP: "The Lord your God is one God!"
ASSIGNMENT: Read pages 10-16, *The Kingdom*. <u>Bible - Matthew 1-28</u>. Read four chapters daily. Draw Scripture from Scripture Box. Remember Scribe Page.
READ: The Narrow Gate Matthew 7:13-14 It is a narrow way through which we enter God's Kingdom. It is a particular path to walk. The Believer's Manifesto the class has written is a clear signpost to the Kingdom pathway.
CLOSE: The Lord's Prayer Place your hand on the heart of each person praying that their heart will learn the way to God and they will truly become HIs Kingdom people.

SESSION TWO The Kingdom page 11-16, Kingdom TM page 26, Kingdom Journal page 26

Theme: The Statement of Belief - The Believer's Manifesto
Activity: Polishing the Statement and Writing the Addendum
Resources: The Apostles' Creed, Whiteboard

<u>Introduction:</u> **The Statement of Faith** Initial statements, at this point, are still open for questions and clarification to all. Once all discussion is finished and all fine points agreed upon, then you can vote on the finished product. Once the statements have been accepted then the Believer's Manifesto can be transferred neatly to a single page inside *The Revolution Begins- The Journal of Kingdom Dreams, Visions and Blueprints*, page 26.

After finishing these statements review part two through part three of chapter two, covering angels to eternity. Generate ideas to include any subjects necessary as an addendum to their manifesto. Jot down important thoughts and ideas on the whiteboard to include as an addendum to the initial statement. Share ideas until you have distilled thoughts into two to three sentences. The addendum can be included at the end of the first statement. Write the addendum on page 26 of their Journal - *The Revolution Begins*. Have one person read aloud the completed version of the statement from last session with these sentences added. Begin with, "We believe."

Activity: The Apostles' Creed Share a statement of belief written by the early church fathers - *The Apostles' Creed*. A copy of this creed is included in *The Kingdom Teacher's Manual,* page 26. Do not allow the word catholic to be confusing. This is a creed written in early church beginnings and currently used in a wide variety of Christian churches. The term catholic, spelled with a small c, means universal. In some churches the word Christian replaces the word catholic.

The Apostles' Creed is a composite statement of belief of the early church. This creed contains the very basic, foundational statement of the Christian faith - the core doctrine of belief for Christians.

Discussion: 1. Why would a creed be important? 2. Why did the early church form a creed? (Only the rich or the scholars could read and not many copies of the Bible existed. What copies of the Bible did exist were hand-copied versions. The common people needed to know the core of the faith so that they would not fall into heretical doctrine.) Finalize any additional comments the class may want to include in their foundational statement after hearing and reviewing a copy of *The Apostles' Creed*.

WRAP: Again read aloud the founding statement the class has composed. Post this copy of the creed written by the class and also a copy of *The Apostles' Creed* so it can be seen for the whole of the study.

ASSIGNMENT: Draw from Scripture Box. Remind everyone to write on their Scribe Page. Read 17-18, *The Kingdom*. <u>Bible - John 1-21.</u> Read three chapters daily.

READ: Parable of the Net Matthew 13:47-50. **Sheep and Goats** Matthew 25:31-46

CLOSE: The Lord's Prayer Lay your hand on each heart and pray that the eyes of their heart will be open so they can see God's Kingdom before them.

Chapter Three   THE TRUE AND FAITHFUL KING

SESSION ONE   The Kingdom pages 17-18, Kingdom Journal pages 21, 27-32

Theme: The King's Invitation
Activities: The Invitation and The Wise Little King Play
Resources: Heart Invitations, copies of the play, play props.

<u>Introduction</u>:   What does it mean to give your life to Jesus? This session tackles this key issue and facilitates the move to absolute surrender.

<u>Talking Point:</u> **The King's Invitation** *"It is through one man's disobedience (Adam) that sin came into the world and the obedience of one man (Jesus) that we are justified and brought back to life (Romans 5:12-19 also read the footnote). It is by grace we are saved through faith. It is a gift of God not of our own works (Ephesians 2:8-9).* God desires to restore to us His Kingdom."

"Turn to the King's Invitation page 27, *The Revolution Begins*. This is a time of quiet meditation, inviting Jesus to speak to your heart. During this time everyone is to write a response to their invitation page 28. Afterwards we will share responses."

"I invite you to submit your lives, hopes and dreams to Jesus together in the *Prayer of Salvation,* page 18. (Allow quiet meditation and all to acknowledge their new relationship with Jesus before you move from this moment.) Your name is now recorded in a book in heaven called, *The Lamb's Book of Life*." (Fill in information in the front of their Kingdom Journals.) Share what their committment means.

<u>Activity:</u> **The Play - The Wise Little King** This is a play to help all recognize the depth of their commitment. Ask for volunteers to play the different parts: a king, a royal Vizier, Jesus, the royal guard, the King's son and a reader. This is pretend, so use lots of imagination, but do not spend much time on costumes. Set out a big chair and a crown for the king, a hat for the Vizier, and a Cross for Jesus. Play, 29-31, *The Revolution Begins*.

At the end of the play, have all put on a crown and listen to Michael W. Smith's song, *Agnus Dei*. Here all can bow and place their worldy crowns at the feet of Jesus.

<u>Discussion:</u> Each person writes their own responses to the play on *The Wise Little King Worksheet,* or the questions can simply be discussed. Allow time to finish and then share answers. Answers can vary. Generally accept all answers but when there is a better answer amplify it. The following are suggestions: 1. In relationship two there is light in the kingdom, but the king still lives by his own wisdom. The king is still the center of attention. In relationship three, the king abdicates his throne and gives his authority to rule, to Jesus. 2. The little king represents us. 3. The royal Vizier is *our* ego or pride. 4. The royal subjects could be the world, the church, our ego or pride. It is important that we completely submit to Jesus as Lord and Savior. 5. Is that commitment clearer now?

In the final sentence Jesus asks the little king to rule and reign with Him. There were several steps involved in the king moving from the first relationship into the final relationship. First, the king had to let Jesus into his kingdom. Next, he had to have a revelation that Jesus needed to be the one to sit on the throne of this life. And finally, the

king had to bow his knee to Jesus and offer Jesus his earthly crown. We can submit to Jesus, lay down our own will and way and move step-by-step into relationship.
The First Kingdom Quest: God has given us the key to His Kingdom. It is the Cross. The Cross has opened the Kingdom doors to eternity, blessing, hope, peace, well-being, order, happiness, holiness and freedom. Their quest is to find their "special keys" (Cross) to wear or to display. Record Kingdom quest, page 21, *The Revolution Begins.*

WRAP: "Jesus said, *If anyone wishes to come after Me , let him deny himself, and take up his Cross, and follow Me. For whoever wishes to save his life shall lose it; but whosoever loses his life for My sake shall find it* (Matthew 16:24-25). Submitting to Jesus is a life- time Kingdom attitude."
READ: Pearl of Great Price Matthew 13:44-46, **Treasures in Heaven** Matthew 6:19-21
ASSIGNMENT: Read 18-21, *The Kingdom.* Bible - Read Romans 1-16. Reading about 21/2 chapters daily. Remember Scripture Box and Scribe Page
CLOSE: The Lord's Prayer Pray for each heart: Lord, may your Kingdom truly come in this heart! May this heart die to self and embrace the resurrection power of the Cross!

SESSION TWO The Kingdom pages 18-21, Kingdom Journal page 22, 33-36

Theme: The Word of God
Activity: The Shout of Holy
Resources: Four Gospels, Noise Makers, Colored Pencils

Introduction: Jesus our King is the, Word of God, in the flesh. He was with God in the beginning. Read the Creation story, Genesis, Chapters 1- 3. Read John 1:1 - 5. Jesus, the Word of God, became flesh to dwell among us. He is the Light of Life, the Light of Men. The story of His life is told through the four Gospels: Matthew, Mark, Luke and John.
Third Prophetic Action: The Shout of Holy Color the gospels pages 33-36, *The Revolution Begins*. Suggest backround colors: Man-purple, Lion -yellow, Ox-red and Eagle-blue. Hang a copy on each of the four sides of the room. Read aloud, The four Gospels, page 19. Stand with these living words and shout, *"Holy, Holy, Holy, Holy is the Lord God Almighty who was, and is and is to come (Revelation 4:8)!"* Pretend you are standing by the throne of God. Make a loud and joyful noise unto the Lord along with the four Gospels. Record your prophetic action, page 22 *The Revolution Begins.*
Discussion: Share the Crosses they found on their Kingdom quest. What do they mean to each one? Then discuss page 18 - 21 on. 1. How can you know if God is speaking His Word to you? (Ask for personal examples) 2. What is the difference between education with our own minds and education from God? How can we learn and practice education from God? 3. Discuss what it means to be a living Word. 4. What is the difference between logos and rhema? Why is it important to recognize the difference?
Alternate Activity: Choosing the Kingdom A decision has to be made as to which Kingdom a person chooses. They cannot live in the kingdom of this world and the Kingdom of God for God's Kingdom is a holy place. We are not to be of this world! Sometimes this

decision has to be repeated to be reinforced. In my house I have a large rug over the top of my regular carpet. I pretend the rug stands for the world, the carpet stands for God's Kingdom. At one point they must choose to fully stand in God's Kingdom. Have all stand and one-by-one choose God's Kingdom. When all are finished repeat a shout of *Holy*! When we fully choose the Kingdom, God obligates Himself to help us keep our commitment.

WRAP: "Holy! Holy! Holy is the Lord God Almighty who was and is and is to come!"
ASSIGNMENT: Read 21-24, *The Kingdom*. Bible - Mark 1-16. Read 2 -3 chapters daily. Bring food to share a dinner meal. Scripture Box, Scribe page
READ: The Greatest in the Kingdom Matthew 18:2-4
CLOSE: The Lord's Prayer Lay your hands on each heart and pray: Lord, allow the understanding of the holiness of your Kingdom come to this heart!

SESSION THREE The Kingdom pages 21-24, Kingdom Journal page 17,22

Theme: The Contract Signed in Blood
Activities: The Cup of Friendship/Share a meal
Resources: Wine/Grape Juice, (optional) The Highest Bidder tape

Introduction: Discuss and participate in the everlasting, Kingdom contract.
Discussion: The Cup of Friendship - Power in the Blood Read and discuss: *The Contract Signed in Blood, the Cup of Friendship* and *Power in the Blood*, on pages 21 - 24. Discuss the following questions: 1. What are the Old and New Covenants and how are they the same? Different? 2. What does the salvation experience demand? 3. What are our rights and privileges under the New Covenant?
Talking Point: The Kingdom Contract John 6:32-35 "Jesus proclaims Himself the Bread of Life, *He who comes to me will never hunger or thirst."* As we come to Jesus as our, Bread of Life, worldly hungers and thirsts will cease. Unnatural eating habits, cravings for drugs, power, sex and alcohol will no longer control us. His Covenant of His body and His blood is a literal contract on His part to give us physical, spiritual and emotional freedom." Allow quiet time of reflection before offering the Cup of Friendship.
Fourth Prophetic Action: The Cup of Friendship Share a cup of friendship with each other and with Jesus. Christian churches often offer communion. Communion affirms our blood covenant with God. Listen to and sing, *This is the Air I Breathe*- Michael W. Smith
Passover Prayer/Supper: Pray the Passover Prayer, page 24 and record prayer page 17, *The Revolution Begins*. Finish through page 24 in *The Kingdom*. Share your meal.

WRAP: "Jesus offers us an everlasting contract of His love - a contract signed with His body and blood. Remember and participate in this covenant often (Luke 22:17-20)."
ASSIGNMENT: Read 25 - 31, *The Kingdom*. Bible - Luke 1-24. Read 3-4 chapters daily. Mark areas for personal prayer Journal page 17. Scripture Box and Scribe Page.
READ: Parable of Lost Sheep, The Lost Coin and The Lost Son Luke 15:3-32
CLOSE: The Lord's Prayer Pray over each heart:Jesus is the lover of your soul!

Chapter Four   PREPARE FOR THE KINGDOM

SESSION ONE   The Kingdom pages 25-31, Kingdom Journal page 17

Theme: Repentance and Holiness
Activities: Prayers to Repent - Personal and Family

Introduction: Repent, for the Kingdom of Heaven is near! If we are to be a people holy to the Lord, then choices must be continually made. According to Webster's Dictionary holiness is, sacred, sanctified and consecrated. How do we become holy consecrated?

Discussion: Read 1 Corinthians 3:16-17. Discuss the following questions 1. What do you think holiness is? 2. Why would you want to be holy? 3. Now that you belong to God's Kingdom, why is it important to be careful what activities you are involved in? 4. Why do we need to repent?   Look up Romans 1:18-32, Revelation 21:8-9, Deuteronomy 18:9-13. Review these Scriptures in an amplified Bible. Read related footnotes.

Talking Point: Holiness "Those who dishonored God by the way they live were under a curse. (Deuteronomy 27:14-26 and 28:15-20.) Jesus broke this curse as He hung upon a Cross. We can be released from curses as we confess sin, repent of that sin and accept the price that was paid for sin. As we repent we step into holiness. There are two kinds of holiness: the holiness Jesus offers as we choose to repent and holiness that is a growing in sanctification (I Corinthians). We continually choose holiness. Everything in God's Kingdom is holy for God is holy. We cannot treat/handle the holy things of God carelessly."

Activity: Repenting Read and review pages 26-28 in, *The Kingdom*. Have each person make a checklist of any activity they have been involved in that will require prayer. Allow time to repent. Record their list on page 17 of *The Revolution Begins*. You can assign small groups for personal prayer. Make sure each group has mature leadership. Review personal prayer of repentance page 28 *The Kingdom*.

Activity: Breaking Generational Curses from the Family Tree Review pages 29-31. Use the prayer example page 30. Have each person make a list of family sins four generations back. Use page 17 in *The Revolution Begins*. Pray together in small groups.

Activity: Pray for Mercy and Grace The most frequent form of repentance is for mercy and grace. There is no formal prayer, just humble yourself before God. Journal page 17.

Prepare for Baptisms: Introduce what it means to be buried with Christ in water baptism, and what one to expect in the Holy Spirit baptism for the next lesson.

WRAP: "Turn from unholy living and become God's holy people. God is holy! His Word is holy! His Kingdom is holy! You cannot possess the things of the Kingdom unless you practice holiness! Repenting and holiness are life-time Kingdom attitudes!"

ASSIGNMENT: Read 31 - 34, *The Kingdom*. Bible - Acts1-28, seven chapters daily. Water Baptism and the gift of the Holy Spirit will be offered at the next session. Prepare for getting wet. Plan a place to baptize. Remember the Scribe Page and Scripture Box.

READ: The Pharisee and the Tax Collector. Luke 18:9-14 **Judging** John 7:1-6.

CLOSE: The Lord's Prayer Pray over each heart: Lord help this heart to truly desire to walk in holiness.

SESSION TWO The Kingdom pages 31-34, Kingdom Journal page 17

Theme: Be Baptized With Water and the Spirit
Activities: Baptism in Water and Baptism in the Holy Spirit.
Resources: Water Baptism, a Guest Speaker, Whiteboard

Introduction: Water Baptism and Holy Spirit Baptism Just like salvation, both of the baptisms are a matter of choice. Expect profound, supernatural experiences. These experiences may be immediate or revealed over a period of time. With baptism in the Holy Spirit expect speaking in tongues.

△ **Triune Language of God** Begin with an overview on the whiteboard on how God relates to man in Salvation, water baptism and baptism of the Holy Spirit. Draw a triangle.
Talking Point: Triune Language "God is a triune God: Father, Son and Holy Spirit. God has made man in His image. Man is: body, soul and spirit. Place the word physical body on the top point, soul on the left, spirit on the right and place the word, man, in the middle.

"Salvation is for the soul of man. It is the first and necessary experience for the believer - the act of redemption. The soul must be redeemed. Here lies the Kingdom entryway." (Place the words Salvation and Jesus next to the word soul.)

"Water baptism is for the physical man. In baptism we are buried with Christ and arise a new creature. *If we died with Him we shall also live with Him* (2 Timothy 2:11). We no longer live for ourselves(2 Corinthians 5:15). God the Father created man."

"The infilling of the Holy Spirit is for the spirit of man to open man to walk as a spirit-being. Man is a spirit-being to be led only by the Spirit of God. God is spirit and those who worship Him must worship Him in spirit and in truth. Place the words Holy Spirit next to Holy Spirit baptism. (Note: Man is a spirit creature in direct opposition of a world view of man as a physical or sexual creature.)"

"The Holy Spirit inspires, directs, teaches and delivers. Doing good works to please man, or to try to please God, is a worldly pattern. We no longer do works for the sake of works. Rather, we determine to wait for the Holy Spirit's guidance."

"Some churches encourage people to renew their decision for Jesus. Just as that decision can be renewed, so can the decisions made in water baptism and Holy Spirit baptism be renewed."

Teaching: Be Baptized Teaching and testimonies. Baptize participants. Pray for each one to receive the Holy Spirit and speaking in tongues. Review the gifts and fruits of the Spirit (1 Corinthians 12:1-11, Galatians 5:22-23). Record water baptism and Holy Spirit baptism - *The Revolution Begins,* page 17.

WRAP: Share experiences of what God revealed to each in the baptisms.
ASSIGNMENT: Read 35 - 41, *The Kingdom*. <u>Bible - 1 Corinthians 1- 24</u>. Read four chapters daily. Remember Scripture Box and Scribe Page.
READ: The 10 Virgins Matthew 25:1-13 **Ask, Seek, Knock** Matthew 7:7
CLOSE: The Lord's Prayer Pray for each heart: Know and listen to the Holy Spirit!

Chapter Five   THE KINGDOM STANDARDS

SESSION ONE   The Kingdom pages 35-41, Kingdom Journal pages 18, 21-22, 38-39

Theme: Love - The Law of the Kingdom
Activities: Law of Love, Choral reading, Worksheet, The Quest
Resources: Law of Love, Choral Reading, Choice Worksheet

<u>Introduction</u>: Read II Kings 13:15-19 on page 35. Determination and perseverance are necessary factors in living out God's Kingdom. We will practice both to raise the Godly standards: love, faith and hope (1 Corinthians 13:13-14). Lack of perseverance can cause us to lose the victory. You must perservere to obtain the Kingdom!

△ <u>**The Triune Language of God**</u>: **The Three Standards of the Kingdom** In God's Kingdom there are three standards that remain immoveable, they are: love, faith and hope. They are the very essence of the Kingdom.

Draw a triangle on the whiteboard. Top point, God the Father, left point, Jesus the Son, and right point, God the Holy Spirit. Place the word God in the middle of the triangle. Next to God the Son, place the word love. Next to God the Holy Spirit, place the word faith, and next to God the Father, place the word hope. The first lesson of chapter five begins with love, for love is the very heartbeat of the Kingdom and the only Kingdom law.

<u>Discussion</u>: 1. What is Old Testament law? 2. What is New Testament law? The spirit of both old and new law is love. In the Old Testament you could follow the letter of the law but not fulfill the true spirit of the law. In the New Testament the spirit of the law is made clear.

<u>Talking Point</u>: **The Law of Love** Use the Ten Commandments (Exodus 20:1-17) to illustrate how God has taken away our heart of stone and given us a new heart, page 38, *The Revolution Begins*. "God has written His law of love upon our hearts, no longer upon tablets of stone. We obey because it is written on our hearts. We are free to obey out of love. Jesus has taken away our stony hearts (Ezekiel 11:18-20, 36:26-28), and written His love on a new heart - a heart that honors Him. Love is the only Kingdom law."

<u>Activity</u>: Have everyone fill in their commandments from the Old Testament (Exodus 20:1-17), and from the New Testament page 38, *The Revolution Begins*.

<u>Optional Activity</u>: Review the old covenant-*Ten Commandments*, by Cecil DeMill.

<u>Talking Point</u>: **Free Will** "Love is the first and foremost standard of God's Kingdom and the New Testament law of God's Kingdom. God has given you His heart to know love and the freedom to choose love. And God has given you free will - the right to choose."

<u>Discussion</u>: 1. What is free will? 2. How could you misuse such a gift as free will? 3. How have you misused this gift before? 4. Why do you think God gave us a free will? 5. Why is it important that we do not give our free will away to another but that we do give our free will in complete obedience to God?

<u>Talking Point</u>: **Love is a Choice** "Now that the Kingom of love is in your heart, you can choose love and your feelings will follow your choices. That feelings follow choices is a godly concept not compatible with the world's view. It is one of those patterns referred

to in the beginning of *The Kingdom*. Worldly wisdom tells us that if we no longer feel love, then love is gone. In God's Kingdom, love is a choice. You recognize feelings as fickle. Feelings are to follow the choices we make."

Activity: The Choral Reading A choral reading is found on page 39, *The Revolution Begins*. Allow time for a silent read through. Read the poem aloud and assign parts. Recite the choral reading several times. Listen to the sounds the words make where a group reads, where a single voice reads. Discuss the poem and its impact when read as a choral reading.

Discussion: Pages 37-38 1. Name several differences between feelings and love. 2. Do you always ignore feelings? 3. How can you choose to love when you have been hurt? 4. What are the three steps? 5. Why is it important not to forget any steps?

Prayer: Forgiveness Choose love! Fill in the worksheet page 18, *The Revolution Begins*. Write a list of those you forgive.

The Second Kingdom Quest: The Stick of Perseverance Assign a Kingdom quest for the following session. Each person needs to go on a Kingdom quest to find a long, strong stick to bring to class to be used in the next assignment. This stick will be used to beat the ground. It is a stick to keep as a reminder to strike the ground often in love and forgiveness. Record action page 22, *The Revolution Begins*.

WRAP: "The Lord has removed our hearts of stone and forgiven all our sin. As His disciples, we choose to forgive and love others as He forgave us. Our love is limited and conditional, but Jesus dwells in our hearts so we can draw upon His unlimited reservoir of love. Choosing love and forgiveness are life-time Kingdom attitudes! Love is the distinguishing mark of those who follow Jesus (Luke14:25-33)."

ASSIGNMENT: Read 41-51, *The Kingdom*. Bible - 2 Corinthians 1-13, Galatians 1-6. Read about 3 chapters daily. Remember the quest, Scribe's Page and the Scripture Box.

READ: True Discipleship John 13:34-35 **Another Parable** Matthew 13:33-34

CLOSE: The Lord's Prayer Lay your hands on each heart and pray that the Jesus will remove their heart of stone and give them a heart of flesh so they may choose love. Love is the distinguishing mark of those who follow Jesus.

SESSION TWO The Kingdom pages 41-51, Kingdom Journal 18-19,22,39

Theme: Forgiveness - an Act of Love
Activities: Personal Prayer, The Treasure Map, Beating the Ground
Resources: The Treasure Map, Sticks.

Introduction: Repeat choral reading page 39, *The Revolution Begins*.

Prayer: Have participants use their list of those they need to forgive and those who they need to ask forgiveness from page 18, *The Revolution Begins*. Take their time and pray for each person on their list. Sample prayer page 41, *The Kingdom*.

The Fifth Prophetic Action: Strike the Ground Striking the ground is in reference to the introduction to chapter five. (Read page 35 to the top of page 36 together.)

Talking Point: Beat the Ground "In the beginning God owned the ground. But because of the fall man and the resulting curse, the ground is a virtual, supernatural place of spiritual snakes (the enemy - demonic forces). Snakes rob the victory. The king did not beat back all of those those snakes in faith (doubt, fear, indecision) so they cost him victory. Note: Victory can be instantaneous, but is also a matter of learning the ways of God's Kingdom, our willingness to progress and Holy Spirit revelation. Revelation is a continuous process." Record action page 22, in the Kingdom Journal.

"Choose to beat the ground and take back the territory that is rightfully yours! Using a stick, strike the ground often and hard. Kill and drive back those snakes of defeat and take back the ground." In Matthew 11:12 Jesus declares: *From the days of John the Baptist until now, the Kingdom of Heaven has been forcefully advancing and forceful men lay hold of it!"*

"Striking the ground reinforces the attitude of perseverance, determination and choice. It is a physical action whereby we lay hold of the ground in the spiritual before we take the ground in the natural. In this example, we use this action as a physical reminder to choose to perserve in forgiving."

Outside activity: Strike the Ground Literally have everyone beat the ground with their stick! Set hearts to seek forgiveness! Drive out snakes that hinder! Continue until the heaviness lifts. Record their prophetic action on page 22, *The Revolution Begins.*

The Sixth Prophetic Action: Healing the Heart We can be wounded in the supernatural with wounds that cannot be seen with the physical eyes, but truly influence the spirit man. This wounding inhibits our heart from being free. Wounds must be confronted regularly otherwise they fester causing bitterness/anger/grief/torture/rage/intense feelings of revenge. These hidden heart wounds consume our energy and time as we can walk around in self-pity and depression playing the victim or act in spite, in anger or display violent behaviors.

Sometimes just praying for the heart to be healed works. Sometimes our wound is like a knife to the heart or a stab in the back or perhaps, a stone of offense has rolled its way into a relationship. In the supernatural we must deal with the blow that has been sent. If you are aware of a particular incident, act out pulling that knife from your heart, taking the arrow from your back or rolling away the stone of offense. We have literally received a blow in the supernatural from the enemy. We undo that blow by a supernatural action. Jesus paid the price to set us free! *The thief (the snake who robs our peace) comes only to steal and kill and destroy, but I, (Jesus) have come that they may have life and have it to the full (John 10:10).* Record your prophetic action on page 22, *The Revolution Begins.*

"We truly walk as free people in choosing to love. Know this choice opens us up to be hurt again but it also opens our heart to be truly free! Be wise enough not to walk into a situation where people will intentionally use and hurt you. Be aware that some people use hurt to attempt to control. Sometimes it is simply an honest mistake, as we are all very much human. Do not be easily offended. Do not gossip. Amidst it all, walk in wisdom holding forth the willingness to bless and forgive in all circumstances." Lay hands on each others' hearts praying God give each heart wisdom in relationships and that each heart journeys with godly wisdom (Proverbs 3:5-6, Proverbs 2).

Pray: Discuss materials pages 41-51. Fill in needs for prayers in *The Revolution Begins,* page 18-19. Together pray over individual lists.

Activity: The Kingdom Treasure Map The last lesson and the beginning of this lesson students have been mining the Word of God for treasures of God's Kingdom. Here they are to use their maps as a guide to map Kingdom territory, *The Revolution Begins*, page 44. Using their text, have everyone list thirteen treasures they have unearthed in the area of love. Write the answers on the love wheel on their Kingdom treasure map. Share observations with the class.

Optional Activity: Repeat the choral reading - Love Never Fails, page 39, their Journal.

WRAP: "Love is a choice. We choose to love as God first loved us. Kingdom love is a strong kind of love that demolishes the power of the enemy and frees people. For, *love never fails!* Love and forgiveness are life-time Kingdom attitudes!"

ASSIGNMENT: Read 52-62, *The Kingdom.* Bible - Hebrews 1-13 and 1-2 Timothy. Read seven to eight chapters daily. Write in Scribe's Page. Remember Scripture Box.

READ: The Unmerciful Servant Matt 18:21-35 **Judging Others** John 7:1-6

CLOSE: The Lord's Prayer Lay your hand on each heart and pray: Lord teach this heart to be merciful and practice forgiveness. Let this heart know and practice your love.

SESSION THREE The Kingdom pages 52-61, Kingdom Journal 20,22

Theme: Faith - Kingdom Principles
Activities: Kingdom Map, Speak to Circumstances, Deposit of Faith
Resources: Kingdom Map, Piggy Bank and Coins

Introduction: Faith For this session, faith is mined as a treasure of the Kingdom. Faith is the substance-maker of God's Kingdom. Faith is a choice. One can experience doubt and circumstances can be deceptive but in the middle of it all you can stand, knowing God is in charge, and that He works all circumstances for good for those who love Him. Have everyone look up and read aloud Romans 8:28.

Discussion: Discuss faith in the areas of principles, attitudes and substance pages 52 - 61, *The Kingdom.* Share personal examples or ask others to share.

The Seventh Prophetic Action: Speak to Circumstances *The Kingdom*, page 56. God has given us the authority to command circumstances to be under our feet. We are to walk above the circumstances. Everything is under the feet of Jesus, (Ephesians 1:22) and we are heirs and coheirs with Jesus (Romans 8:12-17).

Have everyone write a personal example of an overwhelming circumstance, then perform this prophetic action. They may literally want to place their list under their feet. You may stand with one person and help them. Orally they are to command their circumstance, in the name of Jesus, to come under their feet. Commands are loud! Remember to persevere! Record experience on page 22, *The Revolution Begins.*

Another approach is to literally take their eyes off circumstances and focus instead on God. Peter had to focus on Jesus when he walked on water. Know that God who created the universe is bigger than all problems in this universe.

The Eighth Prophetic Action The Deposit of Faith Use bank and coins. Have each person deposit coins in the bank. Review faith as substance page 61, *The Kingdom*.
Talking Point: Faith "Where is your change? What good is change when it is in a bank? What does it mean to have a deposit in an account with God? What does it mean for your children? In God's supernatural Kingdom, when you believe, you exercise faith and your Kingdom account receives credit. This account is just like money in a bank for you and your children. Faith makes substance. When you have a need you can go to the bank and make a withdrawal. *Without faith it is impossible to please God, because anyone who comes to Him must believe that He exists and that He rewards those who earnestly seek Him (Hebrews 11:6).* Record Prophetic Action page 22, *The Revolution Begins.* You don't need anything but faith to make substance. Faith is a Kingdom principle."

"Recognize the difference between a law and a principle. In the New Testament Love is the law. If you break this law (choose not to love or forgive) you come under the judgment of God, for, breaking the Law brings judgment. Faith is not based on law, rather on principles. If you choose not to follow a faith principle you have not broken the Law. You will miss pleasing God and you miss out on huge Kingdom blessing. Both are choices but the outcome is different between love (Kingdom Law) and faith (Kingdom principle)."
Discussion: Fill in thirteen examples on the Kingdom maps for the principles of faith. Discuss the principles they find, or you can brainstorm the answers together as you work.
Prayers: *The Kingdom*, 53, 56. Record prayers page 20, *The Revolution Begins*.

WRAP: "When we believe in God we exercise faith. Faith pleases God! Faith makes substance in the Kingdom of God making those things that were not come into being. God rewards those who earnestly seek Him. Choosing faith is a life-time Kingdom attitude!"
ASSIGNMENT: Read pages 62 - 66. Prepare to share Scribe's Page. Bible - Ephesians 1-16, Philippians 1-4 Titus 1-3, Philemon 1. Read eight chapters daily. Scripture Box.
READ: The Parable of the House Built on the Rock Matthew 7:24-27
CLOSE: The Lord's Prayer Heart Prayer: Build on a solid foundation of love and faith.

SESSION FOUR The Kingdom pages 62-66, Kingdom Journal pages 20-22

Theme: The Hope - The Promise of the Kingdom
Activities: The Walk of Signs and Wonders, The Honor Chair
Resources: Kingdom Map, Honor Chair, Colored Pencils

Introduction: Hope God is a God of hope! Hope is the energizing, Kingdom force.
Discussion: Read and discuss pages 62-66 Find thirteen promises of hope and place them on the map. Color love, faith and hope on the Kingdom treasure maps.
The Ninth Prophetic Action: The Walk of Signs and Wonders Review Signs and Wonders on page 64. As an action of faith, have participants walk around loudly claiming signs, wonders, favor and prophecy follow them where ever they walk. Record your prophetic action page 22, *The Revolution Begins*.
Talking Point: Signs and Wonders "The Word of God states signs and wonders follow the believer. So be expecting! (Read Mark 16:15 -18.) Remind yourself and those

around you that you are expectant! Psalm 5:12 states, *For surely, O Lord, you bless the righteous! You surround them with Your favor as with a shield."*

The Tenth Prophetic Action: The Honor Chair Each person is to sit in a chair designated as the *Honor Chair* as everyone gathers around. One-by-one the scribe's notes are to be read aloud concerning the person in the chair. Encourage all to listen to the voice of the Holy Spirit and add anything the Holy Spirit gives them concerning the person in the Honor Chair. This prophetic action teaches and encourages prophecy. Record Prophetic Action page 22, *The Revolution Begins.*

The Third Kingdom Quest: The Stone of Remembrance In this quest each person is to find, a stone of remembrance. In the Old Testament, God would have the Israelites build an altar of stones where God had met with them. Each time the Israelites passed that stone altar they would remember God and the covenant with them (page 21, *The Revolution Begins*). For this quest, each one needs to discover their stone of remembrance to remind them of the point where God has personally met with them in this study. It can be an ordinary river rock, or it could be jewelry, a piece of art or whatever the Lord reveals. Ask the Lord to help them each find their perfect "stone", something physical they can keep. They are to bring their stone to class and be prepared to share what it means to them. What knowledge have they gleaned from their study of love, faith and hope? Record the quest on page 21 of *The Revolution Begins.*

Intercede: Pray for others and our nation, page 20, *The Revolution Begins.*

The Kingdom Review "The Kingdom of God is based on personal relationship to the triune God: Father, Son and Holy Spirit. *Jesus is the way, the truth and the life* (to that relationship) *and no man comes to the Father except through Him* (John 14:6). Jesus opens the doorway to God's Kingdom of Light. In this Kingdom, Angelic forces participate with us in this battle for God's Kingdom."

"In this Kingdom, the Cross of Jesus is the key that opens the Kingdom doorway and the promise of resurrection power. The Cross is literally the key to God's Kingdom. With His blood, Jesus etched on the Cross His everlasting covenant of love for us. The Bible is the living Word of God given to us to understand this blood covenant."

"This holy Kingdom of God has the three standards of love, faith and hope that stand as its foundational pillars. Love is the heartbeat of the Kingdom and the only Kingdom law. In choosing to love, we choose forgiveness, healing and blessing. Faith is the substance-maker of the Kingdom. Faith outlines the principles of Kingdom living. Hope is the promise of God's Kingdom and the Kingdom energizing force. Each is a matter of choice and of knowing and applying godly wisdom."

WRAP: "The Kingdom offers an infinite, endless supply of hope. Choosing hope is a lifetime Kingdom attitude!"

ASSIGNMENT: Read 67 - 76, *The Kingdom.* Bible - James 1-5. Colossians 1-4, 1-2 Thessalonians. Read 2-3 chapters daily. Review Inner Healing. Be prepared to receive prayer for physical and Inner Healing. Scripture Box

READ: Do Not Worry Matthew 6:25-34 **The Beatitudes** Matthew 5:3-12

CLOSE: The Lord's Prayer Pray: I speak an endless supply of hope to this heart.

Chapter Six THE KINGDOM HEALTH PLAN

SESSION ONE The Kingdom pages 67-76, Kingdom Journal pages 24, 40-41

Theme: Healing - The Song of the Kingdom
Activities: Prayer for Physical Healing and Inner Healing
Resources: Whiteboard, Anointing Oil

<u>Introduction:</u> Allow time to share their Stone of Remembrance.

△ **The Language of God: Body, Soul and Spirit** God is a triune God. God has provided three ways to approach healing: body (physical man), soul (inner man) and spirit (spirit man). Draw a triangle. Place the word man in the middle of the triangle. Place the word body on the top of the triangle, soul on the left and spirit on the right.
Talking Point: Body, Soul and Spirit "God created man as body, soul and spirit. Spiritual healing (often termed deliverance) is for the spirit of man. Here, an actual evil entity has been allowed an open door to enter into the spirit of man and influence him." (Place the word, deliverance, by the word spirit.) "This evil entity must be forcibly expelled!" (Note: deliverance on pages 25 through 30. Further deliverance is addressed in *The Power, Christian Primary III*.

"Inner healing is for the soul of man." (Place the word inner healing by the word soul.) "This type of healing deals with choosing love and forgiveness and healing of memories. It heals the wounds of the soul."

"Physical healing is for the body." (Place physical healing by the word body.) "As you lay on hands to pray for physical healing you may experience heat in your hands. The person receiving pray may experience heat traveling through their body. As you pray, look for the power of God to move through you. It is not through your own strength that you heal. Physical healing can also come through healing of the soul or deliverance. Isaiah 53:5-6 reveals, *Surely He took up our infirmities and carried our sorrows ...He was pierced for our transgressions, He was crushed for our iniquities; the punishment that brought us peace was upon Him and by His wounds we are healed.* See Matthew 8:16-17. Fill in the language of God for all the areas in their Kingdom Journals, page 24."
Discuss and Pray: Read together and discuss the ways to receive physical healing and inner healing. You can work together in small groups and pray for each person over the areas noted. Use pages 40 - 41 in *The Revolution Begins* to record information. Be sure each group has knowledgeable leadership. Listen to the voice of the Holy Spirit. Expect healing to begin this day. In the area of healing of memories, thoughts and events requiring prayer can continue to surface for several weeks. Healing is a process!

WRAP: "Jesus heals and sets us free. We need to be a grateful people. Giving thanks and praise are life-time Kingdom attitudes!"
READ: Ten Healed of Leprosy Luke 17:11-19
ASSIGNMENT: Read 67-76. <u>Bible - 1-2 Peter, 1-3 John, Jude.</u> Read 2 -3 chapters daily.
CLOSE: The Lord's Prayer Pray for hearts: Lord help this be a grateful heart!

SESSION TWO

Theme: The Commission
Activities: Blessing, The Great Commission, The Foot Washing

*The final session should be a time for praise and listening to the leading of the Holy Spirit. Allow time for testimonies. Read the parables. Inscribe all prophetic actions on page 22, *The Revolution Begins*. Ask how this study has changed hearts and lives.

The Eleventh Prophetic Action: The Blessing Inscribe blessings to one another, pages 42 - 43, *The Revolution Begins*.

The Twelveth Prophetic Action: The Great Commission Matthew 28:18 - 20 Lay your hand on the heart of each person and pray, The Great Commision. *"Then Jesus came to them and said, All authority in heaven and earth has been given to Me. Therefore go forth and make disciples of all nations, baptizing them in the name of the Father and of the Son and of the Holy Spirit, teaching them to obey everything I have commanded you. And surely I am with you always - to the very end of the age."*

The Thirteenth Prophetic Action: The Foot Washing Ceremony

Jesus came to serve. In rebuking the disciples over a quarrel concerning who would be the greatest Jesus said, *I am among you as one who serves* (Luke 22:27). At the Passover Feast Jesus volunteered to wash the feet of His disciples. A menial task normally performed by a servant. It was a lesson in humility but it also set forth the principle of selfless service that was soon to be exemplified in the Cross. Jesus' life of service cuminated on the Cross (footnote John 13:5). Read aloud John 13:1-17. Have a foot washing. Reread John 13:13-17. This is the heart of the Gospel message!

Talking Point: Live the Relationship "Doing good works to please man or to please God, is a worldly pattern. God does not call us to works. Rather live in relationship with God and be His child. *To all who received Him, to those who believed in His name He gave the right to become children of God - Children born not of natural descent, nor of human decision or a husband's will, but born of God!"* John 1:12-13.

WRAP: The Seal of the Holy Spirit "Now live your life guided only by the Holy Spirit *and, may the grace of the Lord Jesus Christ, the Love of God, and the fellowship of the Holy Spirit be with you always* (II Corinthians 13:14). And, may signs and wonders confirm the work of the Holy Spirit in your life!

READ: Vine and Branches John 15:1-17. **Be Salt and Light** Matthew 5:13-16

ASSIGNMENT: Bible - Revelation 1-22. Read 3 chapters daily. When you finish reading Revelation you have read through the entire new Testament, Genesis and half of Exodus.

CLOSE: The Lord's Prayer Thank Jesus for His covenant of everlasting love and His gift of the Holy Spirit. Bless each servant's heart to go forth to teach the Kingdom of God!

*This may be an opportunity to continue by studying in this series: *The Glory- Christian Primary II*, and finally, *The Power-Christian Primary III*. *The Kingdom* addressed the issue of who God is and how to establish a solid relationship with Him. *The Glory* concerns man, his anointing, and color and numbers. *The Power* concerns the gifts and fruits of the Holy Spirit and deliverance.

Teacher's Manual Supplementary Packet

		<u>Pages</u>
Chapter One	The Names of God	23
	The Scribe Page	25
Chapter Two	The Apostles' Creed	26
Chapter Three	The King's Invitation	27
	Play: Wise Little King	29
	Wise King Worksheet	32
	The Man - Book of Kells	33
	The Lion - Book of Kells	34
	The Ox - Book of Kells	35
	The Eagle - Book of Kells	36
Chapter Five	Love is a Choice	37
	The Law of Love	38
	Love never Fails	39
	Kingdom Map	40

Teacher's Manual Supplementary Packet

		Pages
Chapter One	The Names of God	23
	The Scribe Page	25
Chapter Two	The Apostles' Creed	26
Chapter Three	The King's Invitation	27
	Play: Wise Little King	29
	Wise King Worksheet	32
	The Man - Book of Kells	33
	The Lion - Book of Kells	34
	The Ox - Book of Kells	35
	The Eagle - Book of Kells	36
Chapter Five	Love is a Choice	37
	The Law of Love	38
	Love never Fails	39
	Kingdom Map	40

The Names of God
God the Father

- **Yahweh YHWH** (comes from a verb which means "to exist) The original Hebrew text was not vocalized, as the name of God was considered too sacred to vocalize.
- **I AM** is derived from the verb "to be" and implies that God is eternal and absolute.
- **Our Father** The Lord's Prayer. Matthew 6:9-13
- **Holy One of Israel**   God is the Holy One of Israel. Isaiah 43:14
- **Yahweh (or Jehovah) Maccaddeshcem** The Lord your Sanctifier. Exodus 31:13
- **The God of the Old and New Testaments** The God of Covenant
- **Elohim** means three-in-one and refers to the triune nature of God. Isaiah 54:5 Genesis 1:1
- **Yahweh (or Jehovah) Ro'i**   Jehovah is my Shepherd. Psalm 23
- **Yahweh (or Jehovah) Jireh** means the Lord Provides. Genesis 22:14
- **El Shaddai** God's name when He appeared to Abraham. It means God Almighty. Genesis 17:1, 28:3 Exodus 6:3
- **Yahweh (or Jehovah) Shalom**   The Lord is Peace.
- **Creator** Genesis Chapter 1
- **Yahweh (or Jehovah) Nissi** The Lord is my Banner - the rallying point and means of victory. Exodus 17:15
- **Yahweh Sabbaoth** means the Lord of Hosts   I Samuel 1:3
- **Yahweh (or Jehovah) Tsidkenu** The Lord our Righteousness. Jeremiah 23:6

The Lord our God is one God. God is spirit and those who worship Him must worship Him in spirit and in truth. He is holy, righteous, omnipresent (always present), omnipotent (all powerful), just and worthy of trust. He rewards the righteous and judges the wicked.

- *Names of God the Father - The God of the Bible, An Introduction to the Doctrine of God, by Robert Lightner, Baker House, Grand Rapids, 1973 page 107-109.*

God the Son

- **Son of God** Opening verse of the Gospel of Mark
- **Jesus** Jesus - the Greek form of Joshua. It means, the Lord saves. Matthew 2:1 Luke 2:21
- **Christ** Luke 24:25
- **Son of the Most High** Luke 1:32
- **The Light of the World** John 8:12 John 12:46
- **The Resurrection and the Life** John 11:25
- **The Lion of the Tribe of Judah**   Revelation 5:5
- **Bread of Life** At the Lord's Supper and John 6:32
- **The Lamb of God who takes away the sins of the world** John 1:29
- **The Lamb** Revelation 5:11-12 **Lamb of God** John 1:29 Revelation 5:6
- **High Priest** Jesus as High Priest appears 10 times in the Book of Hebrews
- **Captain of the Hosts of Heaven, Faithful and True** Revelation 19:11-14
- **The Deliverer** Romans 11:26

- Savior Luke 2:11 **The True Vine** John 15:1-17
- **Wonderful Counselor, Mighty God, Everlasting Father, Prince of Peace** Isaiah 9:6
- **King of Kings and Lord of Lords**   Revelation 19:16
- **Servant** Philippians 2:7 Mark 10:45
- **Son of Man** Jesus used this term when referring to Himself Mark 12:8
- **The Last Adam** 1 Corinthians 15:45
- **Lord of the Sabbath**   Luke 6:5
- **Emanuel** Meaning God with Us   Isaiah 7:14
- **Son of David, Lord** Matthew 21:9 Acts 2:36, Romans 10:9
- **The Word**   John 1:14
- **Teacher** Luke 7:40
- **The Nazarene** Luke 24:19
- **Mediator between God and man** 1 Timothy 2:5
- **The Alpha and the Omega, The Almighty**   Revelation 1:8, 21:6, 12-13
- **The First, the Last, the Living One** Revelation 1:17-18
- **The Amen, The ruler of God's Creation**   Revelation 3:14

Jesus holds the offices of Prophet, Priest and King. Jesus is the only way through which man may be saved. Much of the teaching of Jesus was conveyed through parables. These parables were often comparisons stating, The Kingdom of God is like or, the Kingdom of Heaven is like.

God the Holy Spirit

- **The Truth**   John 16:13-15
- **The Dove**   Matthew 3:16   **Living Water** John 7:37-39
- **The Breath, The Wind**   Genesis 2:7, Acts 2:2
- **The Promise of the Father** Luke 24:49
- **The Oil** Luke 4:8 Acts 10:38
- **Fire for Purification**   Matthew 3:11
- **The Teacher**   John 14:25   **Counselor** John 14:15-16
- **The Deliverer**   He brings His Gifts   1 Corinthians 12:14
- **The Power from on High** Luke 24:48-49
- **We are His Temple** 1 Corinthians 6:19
- **Through Him dwelling in us the fruit of the Spirit is revealed** Galatians 5:22-23
- **He recalls to our mind all that Jesus has said**   John 14:25-25

The Holy Spirit is the Biblical voice of the king, priest and prophet. He is the earnest or guarantee of all God has for us (2 Corinthians 1:22). The Holy Spirit appears in the beginning (Genesis 1:2), in the Old Testament through kings, priests and prophets, God pours out His Spirit on the Church (Acts 2), and in the last days God will pour out His Holy Spirit on all men (Joel 2:28-29).

The Scribe Page

THE APOSTLES' CREED

I believe in God the Father, Almighty
Maker of heaven and earth.
And I believe in Jesus Christ, His only Son our Lord,
Who was conceived by the Holy Spirit,
Born of the Virgin Mary,
Suffered under Pontius Pilate,
Was crucified, died and was buried.
He descended into hell.
The third day He rose again from the dead;
He ascended into heaven,
And sits at the right hand of God the Father, Almighty.
He will come again to judge the living and the dead.
I believe in the Holy Spirit
The holy catholic church,
The communion of saints,
The forgiveness of sins,
The resurrection of the body,
And life everlasting.

The Apostles' Creed, underlining the triune nature of God, appears to be the oldest creed. Legend has it that it was formed by the first Apostles, hence the name. However, there appears to be no direct evidence that this was actually framed by the early Apostles. But the roots of this creed do emulate from the earliest teachings of the church.

The uncaptilized word catholic means universal. In some Christian churches the word catholic is replaced with the word Christian. The line, the communion of saints, refers to the unity and oneness of the body of believers as they become one in baptism, the Lord's Supper and marriage. The word, *saints*, is a reference to all Christians.

The Creed, published by Twenty-Third Publications, Mystic Connecticut, 1987, Bernard L Marthaler, Library of Congress Number 80-50-891, Pages 5, 347-362.

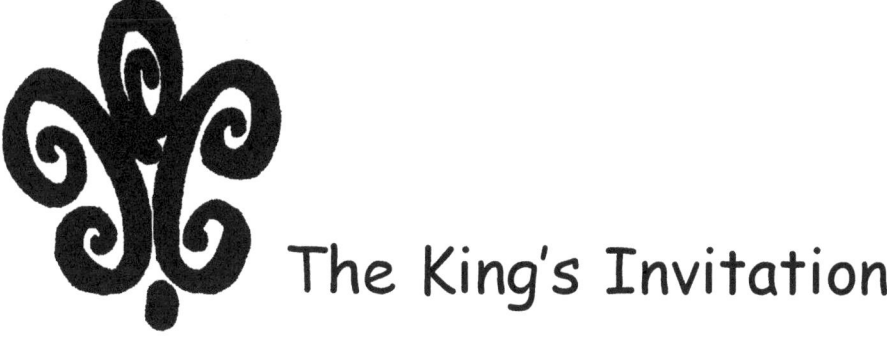

The King's Invitation

Come to Me if you are weary and burdened and I will give you rest. Take My yoke upon you and learn from Me, for I am gentle and humble of heart and you will find rest for your soul.

I am the light of the world. If you follow Me you will never walk in darkness but will have the light of life.

Believe in Me and you will be saved. I am the Resurrection and the Life. He who believes in Me will never die.

Jesus

Our Response to the Invitation

Lord, Jesus forgive my sin, come into my heart. Be my Lord and Savior.

The Wise Little King

Once upon a time there lived a king thought to be very wise. This king had many wonderful treasures. His most prized possession of all stood in the very center of the Kingdom, in the very heart of his castle. This treasure was a great, glittering, jewel-covered, golden throne. The King loved to sit upon his glittering throne wearing his golden crown.

The king adores his lovely throne so very much that he rarely leaves his throne for any reason. He eats there, he drinks there, he even sleeps there. He literally lives upon his royal throne. Because the king sleeps upon his royal throne, he issues this royal degree to be proclaimed through out his kingdom: Whenever the king sleeps, no one is to move or make even the slightest sound to disturb him. Even the royal builders in charge of constantly enlarging his throne room are to stop their work.

Well, one most ordinary day, as the king dozes upon his royal seat, the Commander of the Guard comes rushing into the throne room.

Royal Guard: (A royal guard enters and bows before the sleeping king.) Awake! Awake my Lord!

King: What, what is all the noise about? (The king sputters coming out of his sleep.) Whatever could be such an emergency that you would break the royal decree and rouse my royal wrath?

Royal Guard: Forgive me! Forgive me Majesty! We have a most determined stranger knocking at the castle door.

King: A stranger you say? Send him away! You know no one is to disturb my royal naps!

Royal Guard: Please have mercy on me, great one. We truly tried to rid the kingdom of this stranger but he just keeps knocking and knocking and knocking! He's been knocking for hours! And since it is your royal decree that no one, but no one, is to disturb the royal kingdom during your royal naps we feared what he might do if we open the door. He insists he will continue knocking until the door is opened or He personally hears from you!

Reader: The king is unsettled by the tenacity of the stranger at the door. Who dare ignore his royal decree? Who would be willing to face his royal wrath! A friend? A foe?

King: (The king strokes his royal chin thoughtfully.) Humm! I can see I will have no peace until I face this stranger myself. The king rises from his throne and waves to the guard to lead the way. Together they proceed out of the throne room, past the great dinning hall and through the huge foyer to the castle door. As the king approaches the great door he hears the repeated knock, knock, knocking.

King: Who knocks upon my door? Friend or foe!

Jesus: It is I Jesus! I have been knocking at the door to your kingdom for a great, long time! Will you let me in?

King: Jesus! Many of my royal subjects, including the beggar who sits at the castle gate, have spoken highly of you and all the good you do! Surely I am privileged you have come for a visit!

Reader: The king motions for the royal guard to unlatch the door. The door swings open and Jesus stands before the king.

King: Well, what are you waiting for?

Jesus: An invitation to your kingdom.

King: Come in. Come in! I am so pleased to have you drop by.

Reader: Jesus steps into the kingdom and at that moment the entire kingdom is suddenly filled with light (turn on overhead light in the room). Even the king has a sudden glow about him. For several days thereafter, the only thing kingdom subjects think or talk about is Jesus and the coming of the great light. But business of the kingdom goes on and soon there are other things the center of royal attention, especially with the on-going work of expanding the throne room. This day the royal builder must have the king's ear as he bows before the king with a large scroll in hand.

The Royal Architect: Your Majesty, today laboring on the throne room, workers discovered this ancient manuscript. (The architect hands the king the scroll.)

King: *Thou shall have no other gods before me.* For heavens sakes, what can such a strange thing mean? I must summon my most knowledgeable and trustworthy advisor, the royal Vizier!

The Reader: The king pulls on a long cord.
Sound Effects: Dong! Dong! Dong! (Noise from a loud bell.)

Royal Vizier: Vizier, wearing a tall hat, scurries into the throne room and bows to the king.

King: Tell me, learned one who has studied all the knowledge of my kingdom and all the knowledge of the world, what do these great words upon this scroll mean?

Royal Vizier: (The Vizier ponders the manuscript thoughtfully.) These words are most fitting, your majesty. Your great generosity is known both far and wide - your kindness to the end of the kingdom. How you have shared your leftovers with the beggar who sits by the door is truly retold by all your royal subjects. You really do not have the time to worship other gods with all your good deeds, and then, too, working on enlarging your royal throne room takes the rest of your time. And look at your great kindness in inviting Jesus into your kingdom to live in your presence.

Reade: Well, the king is about to burst his royal buttons! He had not considered his royal greatness. But now that Vizier mentioned it, he was pretty wonderful.

Jesus: (At that very moment Jesus enters the room hand-in-hand with a young child.)

Vizier: (The Royal Vizier turns and nods towards Jesus) Why not allow Jesus an opportunity to speak, my Lord. Especially since it is through your own special invitation that he is even in your kingdom.

King: Come closer, Jesus. This ancient manuscript states, *Thou shall have no other gods before me.* What do you believe it means?

Child: (The child steps forward to speak). Can't you see? Jesus is God. Jesus should sit in the big chair and wear the crown. He deserves to be worshiped.

Vizier: Now, child! (The royal Vizier tries to hustle the child out of the throne room.)

King: Stop! Do not take away the child! The words from the child are true! I have been so blinded by my own importance. (The king moves from his throne and bows at the feet of Jesus.) Truly I am the one needing forgiveness! It is you who should be sitting upon this throne and rule my life. I have taken the honor and glory that belongs to you. I have sat in the place that should have been His alone! I have been running my kingdom my way. I see now this is the wisdom from the ancient manuscript. I set myself to be worshiped as god taking the rightful place that belongs to you. Forgive me! I offer you all I have, my throne and my crown.

King: (The king turns and addresses his royal subjects). Declare from this moment forward that all royal subjects, including the royal Vizier, now and forever more are to kneel and worship before the rightful King upon the throne!

Reader: As all royal subjects, including the humbled king, kneel before Jesus, there is heard a great rejoicing in heaven that day, as a great multitude from every nation, tribe, people and language fall down on their faces, and lay their crowns before the throne (including the wise little king) and worshiped God. They cried with one loud voice as the king lays his earthly crown before the throne!

ALL: (Loud) Praise and glory and wisdom and thanks and honor and power and strength be to, the One seated upon the throne, and to our God forever, and ever, Amen! (Repeat all three times).

MUSIC Music of worship around the throne of God.

Jesus: (Jesus motions for all to be silent. He offers His hand to the kneeling king.) Arise, my son, for you truly are wise. Because you have given Me your kingdom, throne and crown, I offer you my friendship and the keys to my Kingdom (Jesus offers the king His Cross). You are truly worthy to rule and reign with Me for eternity.

The Wise Little King Worksheet   (optional)

1. There are three relationships the king has with Jesus. The first one is when Jesus is at the door knocking. Jesus is outside the kingdom. It is difficult to hear what Jesus is saying. There is no light in the kingdom. What are the two other relationships the king has with Jesus?

2. Who is the wise little king?

3. Who is the Royal Vizier?

4. Who are the royal subjects?

5. Why is it important that the royal subjects bow down?

6. What is the relationship the king has with Jesus in the final sentence?

7. How did the king get from Jesus knocking at the door to the king laying down his throne and his earthly crown for Jesus? How can we get there?

The Man, Symbol of St. Matthew, The Book of Kells

The Lion, Symbol of St. Mark, The Book of Kells

The Ox. Symbol of St. Luke. The Book of Kells

The Eagle, Symbol of St. John, The Book of Kells

Love is a Choice

CHAPTER FIVE   Fill in the worksheet together.

God gives us new _____ where he writes His _____ of _____. God also gives the gift of _____.

Free will is the _____ of choice. With our free will we can make good _____ or we can make _____ choices. We are never to give our _____ over to another. We use our free will _____ when we make The Kingdom choice to _____ and to _____ others.

Love is a _____. Love is a _____. Love is a _____.

Our _____ follow the _____ we make. Our _____ will follow our decision to forgive. Feelings are only _____ and they can _____ us at times. Therefore, we are not to totally _____ upon our feelings.

Feelings can _____ us in relationships or remind us to take care of our _____ _____. Strong feelings need to be acknowledged and not stuffed down or they can cause unresolved anger and depression.

There are three steps to the forgiving process. They are:

1

2

3

The Law of Love

I.

II.

III.

IV.

V.

VI.

VII.

VIII.

IX.

X.

Love the Lord your God with all your heart
With all your soul and with all your mind.
And love your neighbor as yourself.

LOVE NEVER FAILS

Choral Reading I Corinthians 13:1-7 Divide into two groups and a reader. Group A reads, "Love is patient, love is kind." Group B reads, "Love never fails." Single reader reads all first lines in the middle of the poem. And three lines, "But have not love," and the very last word, "life." Create contrasts grouping male voices and female voices or younger voices and more mature voices. Speak with expression and emotion.

Group A:	If I speak in the tongues of men and of angels
Reader:	*But have not love,*
Group C:	I am only a resounding gong or a clanging cymbal!
Group B:	If I have the gift of prophecy and can fathom all mysteries
	And all knowledge, and if I have faith that can move mountains,
Reader:	*But have not love,*
Group C:	I am nothing!
Group A:	If I give my possessions to the poor,
	Surrender my body to the flames,
Reader:	*But have not love,*
Group C:	I am nothing!
Reader	Love does not envy, does not boast.
Group A/C	**Love is patient, love is kind! Love is patient, love is kind!**
Reader	Love is not proud, it is not rude.
Group A/C	**Love is patient, love is kind! Love is patient, love is kind!**
Reader	Love is not self-seeking nor is love not easily angered.
Group A/C	**Love is patient, love is kind! Love is patient, love is kind!**
Reader	Love keeps no records of wrongs.
Group A/C	**Love is patient, love is kind! Love is patient, love is kind!**
Group B	Love never, ever fails!
Reader	Love does not delight in evil, but rejoices with the truth!
Group A/C	**Love is patient, love is kind! Love is patient, love is kind!**
Group B	Love never, ever fails!
Reader	Love protects, trusts, hopes and always perseveres!
Group A/C	**Love is patient, love is kind! Love is patient, love is kind!**
Group B	Love never, ever fails!

Everyone: God so loved the world that He gave His only Son that whosoever **(quiet)**, whosoever **(medium)**, whosoever **(loud)** believes in Him shall not perish but have Everlasting **(quiet)**, Everlasting **(medium)**, Everlasting **(loud)**, Everlasting **(very loud!!)**
Reader: Life!

LEGEND

— ENTER THE KINGDOM —

Enter bottom left into the pure, clear, crystal river of God flowing from the Throne of God. Color, then list 13 examples around each Kingdom treasure. If you can't fit thirteen standards in the area provided, list extras on the back of the map.

LOVE - KINGDOM LAW
I am the Heartbeat
of God's Kingdom.
Color - Red

HOPE = KINGDOM PROMISE
I am the Energizing Force
of God's Kingdom.
Color - Yellow

FAITH = KINGDOM PRINCIPLES
I am the Substance-Maker
of God's Kingdom.
Color - Blue

SONGS OF THE KINGDOM

Healing and Deliverance
Mercy and Grace
Wisdom
Praise and Worship

MAY the Lord bless and defend you.
MAY you find favor in His sight.
MAY you know His love and
MAY you ever dwell, safe by His side.

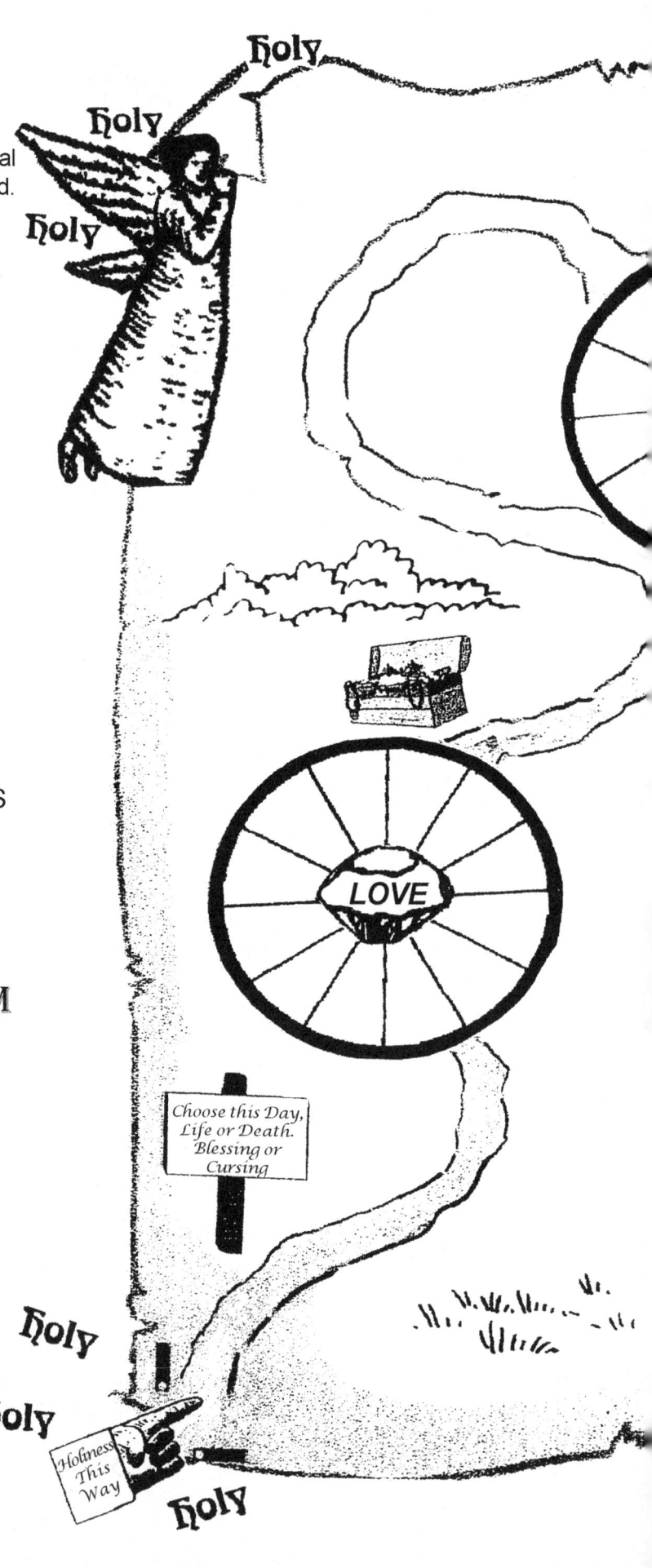

THE KINGDOM

TABLE OF CONTENTS

13+ Kingdom Prayers
A Word from the Author

CHAPTER ONE	THY KINGDOM COME	
	Kingdom Thinking	2
	The Kingdom and You	4
CHAPTER TWO	THE EVERLASTING KINGDOM	
	Triune God	7
	Angels	11
	Eternity	12
CHAPTER THREE	THE TRUE AND FAITHFUL KING	
	Jesus	17
	The Word of God	18
	The Contract Signed in Blood	22
CHAPTER FOUR	PREPARE FOR THE KINGDOM	
	Repent	25
	Generational Forgiveness	28
	Grace and Mercy	30
	Be Baptized	31
CHAPTER FIVE	THE KINGDOM STANDARDS	
	Strike the Ground	35
	Love -The Law of the Kingdom	36
	Faith - Kingdom Principles	52
	Hope -The Promise of the Kingdom	61
CHAPTER SIX	THE KINGDOM HEALTH PLAN	
	Joy and Wisdom as Medicine	67
	Healing for the Physical Body	68
	Healing for the Soul	69
	Healing for the Spirit	75

13+ Kingdom Prayers

*Ask and it shall be given to you.
Seek and you shall find.
Knock and the door will open.*
  Matthew 7:7

THE LORD'S PRAYER	14
THE PRAYER OF SALVATION	18
THE PASSOVER PRAYER	24
PRAYER TO REPENT: Self and Family	28, 30
PRAYER FOR THE HOLY SPIRIT	32
PRAYER OF FORGIVENESS	41, 49
PRAYER OF BLESSING	48
BREAKING SOUL TIES	50
BREAKING JUDGMENTS AND CURSES	51
PRAYER OF FAITH	53
SPEAKING TO CIRCUMSTANCES	56
PRAYER FOR PHYSICAL HEALING	68, 69
INNER HEALING AND DELIVERANCE	74, 75

A Word from the Author

Behold The Kingdom

Jesus teaches us to pray to God and the Father for the Kingdom of God to come and God's will to be done on earth as it is in heaven (Matthew 6:9-15). The founding principle and major premise of this Kingdom is love; God so loved the world that He gave His Son, Jesus. Jesus so loved that He freely offered His life, shedding blood, to pay the price for sin. Then, Jesus sent to all believers His Holy Spirit. God, in His triune nature of Father, Son and Holy Spirit, reveals the Kingdom of God.

Because it is a supernatural Kingdom, understanding this Kingdom cannot be acquired through natural means nor from the perspective of wordly teaching. In God's Kingdom, it is necessary to rely on the gift Jesus gives to all believers: The Holy Spirit, the only spirit-guide to all truth.

You have been chosen, called by name from the time of your conception, to enter this Kingdom of God, where God the Father, Jesus and the Holy Spirit have a plan for your life. Before you awaits this plan to establish hope and a future and to set you free in body, soul and spirit. *The Kingdom - Christian Primary I*, is designed as a blueprint - a blueprint for securing God's Kingdom and your freedom!

My intent in writing *The Kingdom - Christian Primary I* is to map the basic truths of the Christian faith, to establish the entry way and perimeters of God's Kingdom and to impart the Kingdom standards of love, faith and hope. The text is written in a specific order for reasonable progression and includes teachings, directions, sample prayers and personal experiences.

This text is not intended to cover everything a Christian should know or believe, nor is it final or complete. Other Christian authors have written volumes on topics which are covered here in just a paragraph or two. Learning and applying these Kingdom truths takes time and the guidance of the Holy Spirit.

Throughtout the text the terms, the Kingdom of God, the Kingdom of Heaven, God's Kingdom, and the Kingdom of Light are used interchangeably. Whenever it is in reference to God's Kingdom the word Kingdom is always capatilized. All direct Scripture quotes are in italics.

It is with great shout of thanksgiving that I dedicate this series to my Father God who loves me, Jesus, my friend and advocate, and the Holy Spirit, my beloved teacher. I wish to thank Dean and Wayne McPeak, Living Water's prayer group, Jean Rudy, Angie Nuxoll and Tammy Dickson for their faithfulness. Thanks also to Jenny, Cindy and the many others who encouraged me along the way. With special appreciation to Reverend John Sandford who first introduced me to Inner Healing.

This book is my story, my journey to freedom and the truths that released the Kingdom of God into my life and set me free! These truths are truly Kingdom treasure. Into your hands and heart I pour these treasures of God's Kingdom.

I pray that *the eyes of your heart be enlightened, in order that you may know the hope to which He has called you, the riches of His glorious inheritance in the saints, and His incomparably great power for us who believe (Ephesians 1:18 - 19)*.

For the Kingdom,
Ginny

1
Thy Kingdom Come

In the beginning, God creates the heavens and the earth, plants and the beasts. Out of the dust of the earth He forms man and woman in His own image, breathes on them His breath of life and imparts to them dominion over all the earth. The Creator calls all He has made - good. Perfect created beings dwell in perfect created order with their God.

But man, in his conceit, forsakes God and chooses rather to listen to a wicked lie from a fallen angel. A portal of evil opens wide and disgorges its kingdom of lies, shame, fear and curses over innocent creation (Genesis chapter 1-3). Mankind literally steps out of the Kingdom of God into a kingdom of darkness thereby forfeiting relationship with God and dominion over the earth.

And so there became two kingdoms: the Kingdom of God and of Light and the kingdom of lies and of darkness. Between the two kingdoms stands a great, impassable chasm.

But this Creator God is a God of pure love. His love is so enormous He provides an outrageous plan to save mankind. His Son, Jesus, is to offer up his blood on a Cross as the perfect sacrifice. The Cross of Jesus becomes the bridge for man to walk back across that impassable chasm into God's Kingdom. Then mankind and God can again embrace in friendship and man's dominion over the earth can be restored.

KINGDOM THINKING

When we turned our backs on God, we received in exchange the kingdom of darkness. This darkness has its own set of standards. These standards are the complete opposite of the values of God's Kingdom. Now this kingdom of darkness establishes the value system in this world, and because of our darkened understanding we often incorporate this system as truth.

God has a heavenly Kingdom and He wishes this Kingdom to be established so that once again His will can be done on earth as it is in heaven. We can only reestablish this Kingdom by entering into intimate relationship with God the Father, Son and Holy Spirit.

God offers us a picture of His Kingdom through the Biblical types from the Old Testament and in the New Testament through the words and life of Jesus and His followers. In the Old Testament God established Kingdom and favor relationships with Israel through the sacrifical offering for sin with the blood of an innocent lamb. In the New Testament, God the Father sends His only Son, Jesus, as the final and complete blood offering for sin for every man, woman and child that will ever exist.

Our relationship is no longer automatic because of the fall of man, but rather one we must choose to accept. As we enter God's Kingdom, we do not understand how to successfully live His Kingdom and receive full benefits because of our past familiarity with sin, self-dependence and negative thinking ingrained from birth.

To understand God's Kingdom, we turn to God and choose His Kingdom way of thinking, for God emphatically states in His Word:

"My thoughts are not your thoughts, neither are My ways your ways. As the heavens are higher than the earth, so are My ways higher than your ways and My thoughts higher than your thoughts (Isaiah 55:8-9)."

Romans 12:2 exhorts, *Do not be conformed any longer to the pattern of this world, but be transformed by the renewing of your mind.*

1 Corinthians 3:18-20 points out, *Do not deceive yourself. If anyone thinks he is wise by the standards of this age, he should become a fool so that he may become wise, for the wisdom of this world is foolishness in God's sight.*

LIVE THE KINGDOM

The Kingdom of God becomes alive, almost electric in and around you, a spiritual place in which you exist, move, are loved and live in relationship. You live out your Kingdom journey surrounded by others on their journey and others in the world. This concept could be compared to the viritual reality of a sophisticated cyber game.

The access code would be your personal relationship with Jesus, the Bible, your tutor program and the Holy Spirit your constant companion and guide. You would have to learn the language of this alternate reality, apply new patterns for problem solving and search diligently to find new keys for understanding. There would be quests designed to cause you to grow in strength, knowledge and maturity: treasure to discover, battles to win, dangerous pits to avoid, enemies to rout, puzzles to solve, territory to own and captives to set free. You would join forces with others on their Kingdom journey, together overcoming forces of evil.

You can compare God's Kingdom to a computer game, but a computer game is not reality at all, only surface entertainment. However, true Kingdom living is the most personal adventure possible. Kingdom living is the binding of your heart in love to Jesus. Nothing satisfies your heart like this personal relationship!

The Kingdom of God is a forever Kingdom. Many worldly kingdoms and philosophies have consumed minds, ruled hearts and persisted for years. They have simply disappeared from the face of the earth - and are now only memories gathering dust in history books.

The Kingdom of God is more real than the concrete under your feet. Concrete may appear solid, but in a few years it will crumble. Communist Russia built and maintained the Berlin Wall to divide the former nations of East and West Germany. This wall appeared solid and foreboding. But in one days' time, and to the surprise and applause of the world, it collapsed.

This world is temporal and forever changing but God's Kingdom existed long before time began. God's Kingdom is from everlasting to everlasting. It is the true reality. This is how the Lord God instructs us:

Stand at the crossroads and look; ask for the ancient paths, ask where the good way is, and walk in it, and, you will find rest for your soul (Jeremiah 6:16).

THE KINGDOM AND YOU ɾA Brief Overview

WHERE IS THE KINGDOM OF GOD?
The Kingdom of God first becomes resident in you (Luke 17:21).

WHO PAID FOR THIS PRIVILEGE?
God so loved the world that He gave His Son, Jesus (John 3:16). Jesus laid down His life on the Cross, offering His Blood as the purchase price to restore our friendship with God (Romans 5:12-21).

WHO IS ELIGIBLE FOR THE KINGDOM?
The opportunity for anyone to enter into the Kingdom of God began the moment Jesus rose from the dead. Jesus opened (a path, a bridge) a door for every person to enter into the Kingdom of God and for everyone in every nation to know God (Luke 24:45-47, Acts 10:44-48).

HOW DO WE ENTER THE KINGDOM?
God offers this Kingdom of Heaven to anyone who will receive it. All who accept Jesus as their Savior can potentially receive all the benefits God's Kingdom has to offer (Ephesians 1:3). It is through the grace of God that this invitation is extended; the privilege cannot be earned - it is a free gift from God (Ephesians 2:8-9). It is free to anyone who will receive it.

WHAT DOES THE KINGDOM OFFER?
The Kingdom provides a relationship with the Godhead and transforming power (II Corinthians 3:18). Jesus forgives our sins (1 John 1:9). We enter into life and fellowship with God for eternity. When our physical body dies we receive a new body and enter heaven (1 Corinthians 15:42-44). We regain the authority lost in the Garden of Eden.

In this Kingdom, we become part of the family of God. We become sons and daughters. A one-to-one speaking and learning relationship with the triune Godhead is established: Jesus as our friend, God as our Father and the Holy Spirit as our counselor/teacher. Others who have had similar experiences can become our Kingdom brothers and sisters (Ephesians 1:4-6).

WHAT ABOUT THE EQUALITY IN THE KINGDOM?

In the Old Testament, Jewish kings, priests and prophets had a special Kingdom relationship. God imparted His divine purpose through them. In the New Testament, Jesus opens the door for everyone - man, woman, child, slave or free. Equality is not struggled for or earned. Equality is already established (Galatians 3:26-28).

WHAT ARE THE FOUNDING PRINCIPLES OF THE KINGDOM?

The founding principles are love, faith and hope. They are the standards upon which God's Kingdom is built. Without love, there is no Kingdom, for it is by love and through love that God's Kingdom is established (I Corinthians 13:1-13).

Love is the primary force and the only law of God's Kingdom; not a wishy-washy kind of love, but a strong, powerful love, the kind of love that lays down its life as a sacrifice for others.

HOW DOES THE KINGDOM ADVANCE?

The Kingdom advances by inviting others to embrace the friendship Jesus offers, (Matthew 28:16-20), practicing His Kingdom for the benefit of others and ourselves (Galatians 5:22-24) and teaching others of the King and His Kingdom (2 Timothy 4:1-2).

HOW SECURE IS THIS KINGDOM?

The Kingdom of God is an unshakable and eternal Kingdom (Hebrews 12:28). In this Kingdom, God offers to mere humans everlasting life (Daniel 7:26-27, Isaiah 55:3, John 3:15-16).

REVIEW AND PROJECT

Chapter One recognizes both worldly patterns of living and patterns of living established by the Kingdom of God. Its premise is that, at times, we live according to worldly standards because these standards are familiar patterns practiced around us almost daily.

Here is the opportunity to move out of the standards set by the kingdom of this world and step into practicing the principles of an actual kingdom called the Kingdom of God. As you choose to enter into a covenant relationship with Jesus as Lord and Savior, you can be truly set free through His Kingdom living.

The following chapters offer a panoramic view of God's Kingdom, its length and breath, height and depth, all the way down to the very fabric of its being. It reviews Kingdom organization, how different elements of God's Kingdom function, how to become part of this eternal Kingdom, the rights and privileges of being a Kingdom friend, practical applications of Kingdom standards of love, faith and hope, along with Kingdom healing and many opportunities for prayer.

Enter now into viewing this Kingdom based on love - the unshakable, eternal Kingdom of the one, true, triune God and let the Kingdom come into your life on earth as it is in heaven.

2
The Everlasting Kingdom

The Kingdom journey begins through understanding the triune nature of one, holy God. God is holy. Holy means He is pure, sacred and deserving of reverence (deep respect).

TRIUNE GOD

God is one, yet He is triune: Father, Son and Holy Spirit. Each part of the Trinity has a different personality, attributes and functions, but there is only one God. This God lives outside of earthly timelines, although He is the Creator of the earth and Creator of time. This God is above and beyond the limits of this world and the limits of all earthly imaginations.

GOD THE FATHER

God the Father is the great I Am, Creator of the Universe, the Holy One of Israel. He is our omnipresent, omnipotent, omniscient, Abba Father who created us in His very image. This eternal God rests upon His sapphire throne surrounded by His rainbow glory. Four living creatures worship Him day and night, night and day (Ezekiel 1:25-28).

Before anything existed He was. He is a spirit being - a living and holy God who desires fellowship with His creation.

- Is One God   Deuteronomy 6:4
- Created the Heavens and the Earth   Genesis 1:1
- Is the only God   John 17:3
- Is living   Jeremiah 10:10   Revelation 4:9
- Reigns   Psalm 9:7, Psalm 47:6-9
- Is Holy and Eternal   Revelation 4:8

Kingdom / 8

- Is love   1 John 4:8; 4:16   His love endures forever   Psalm 118:1-4
- Is almighty   Genesis 17:1
- Inspired every Scripture   2 Timothy 3:16
- His Word stands forever   Isaiah 40:8
- Never sleeps or slumbers   Psalm 121
- Is the source of all creation and all wisdom   Proverbs 8
- Rewards those who seek Him   Hebrews 11:6
- Is awesome   Deuteronomy 7:21, 10:17
- Is righteous   Psalm 11:7
- Judges   Hebrews 12:23
- Is full of compassion   Psalm 116:5-6
- Is jealous and avenging   Nahum 1:2-3
- Tests hearts   I Chronicles 29:17
- Forgives sins   Mark 2:7, 1 John 1:9
- Turns our darkness into light   Psalm 18:28
- Laughs at the enemy   Psalm 2:4
- is a consuming fire   Hebrews 12:28-29
- Disciplines every son (and daughter) He accepts   Hebrews 12:5-6
- Makes all things possible   Matthew 19:26
- Pours out His love   Romans 5:5
- Is faithful   Deuteronomy 7:9
- Does not show favoritism   Romans 2:11
- Loves the world, gave His Son so believers but have eternal life   John 3:16
- Has made us to be heirs and co-heirs with Christ   Romans 8:17

GOD THE SON

Jesus is the only Son of God. Jesus is the Kings of Kings and Lord of Lords, the Savior of the World and the Light of the World, the One who was, and is and is to come, the One who holds the keys to the Kingdom of Heaven (Matthew 16:19) and the keys to Death and Hades (Revelation 1:18) in His hand and our soon coming King. He is the Lamb of God who takes away the sin of the world, our Bread of Life and the Resurrection and the Life. He stands at the right hand of the throne of God the Father (Acts 7:55). God the Father has placed all things under the feet of Jesus, given Jesus all authority, appointed Jesus head of the Church (Ephesians 1:22) and commanded all His angels to worship Jesus (Hebrews 1:6).

Jesus is the Light of the World, and nothing, neither death nor life, angels or demons, the present or the future, any powers, neither height or depth nor anything else in all creation can separate us from His love (Romans 8:38-39).

- One with the Father   John 17:22
- Is part of the Triune Godhead   John 17:21
- Was present at Creation   John 1:1-10, 14
- Is the Light of the World   John 8:12
- The Son of Man   John 3:13 (see footnote)
- The Son of God   Luke 1:30-35   Is God's only Son   John 3:16
- The only way to God the Father   John 14:6
- The only way to Salvation   Acts 4:12
- Our sin offering   Romans 8:3
- Chose us and adopted us   Ephesians 1:4-5
- Is the Word of God   John 1:1-4   Revelation 19:11-16
- Is the Lamb of God that takes away the sin of the world   John 1:29
- Gives eternal life   John 3:16
- Is the Gate   John 10:7
- Our Shepherd   Psalm 23, John 10:4
- Is gentle and humble of heart   Matthew 11:29
- Is the Bread of Life   John 6:35
- Is the Lion of the Tribe of Judah   Revelation 5:5 (see footnote)
- Is the Captain of the Hosts of Heaven   Revelation 19:11-16 (see footnote)
- Is the Resurrection and the Life   John 11:25
- Is the hope of the nations   Matthew 12:18-21
- Heals the sick   Matthew 4:23-24   Commands us to heal   Mark 16:17
- Baptizes in the Holy Spirit   Matthew 3:11
- Is the same yesterday, today and forever   Hebrews 13:8
- Was conceived by the Holy Spirit   Matthew 1:20
- Was born of a virgin   Luke 1:26-35
- Was baptized in the river Jordan by John the Baptist   Mark 1:9
- Was Holy Spirit-empowered, tempted, healed the sick and blind, preached and proclaimed the Kingdom of God   Gospels: Matthew, Mark, Luke, John
- Was buried and rose on the third day, breaking the power of death over mankind   Luke 24:1-7; Luke 24:45-47; 1 John 5:11-12
- Is Alpha and Omega, the First and the Last, the Beginning and the End   Revelation 22:12-13
- Is returning soon   Revelation 22:7,12

THE HOLY SPIRIT

The Holy Spirit is the gift of God to us - the very life-force of God come to dwell within mankind (Acts 1:4). It is through the Holy Spirit that the gifts and the fruits of the Holy Spirit are released though mankind (Romans 12:1-11). These gifts and fruits are the very character of Jesus (Galatians 5:22-23). The Holy Spirit sovereignly determines which gifts each believer receives.

The Holy Spirit is the only Spirit of Truth and the God appointed Teacher - the Revelator of Jesus. He is the Power Force who delivers and sets us free. The Holy Spirit opens our eyes to the nature of God and guides each individually to understand the Scriptures and to call to mind all that Jesus spoke.

It is through the Holy Spirit that signs and wonders are released. The Holy Spirit speaks through Scriptures, prophecies, dreams and visions. He prompts the believer into fresh understanding. He is the mind and heart of God and He gives to those who believe the power and authroity to live the Christ-like experience. The Holy Spirit reveals the truth of the Words of God.

- Is the third person of the triune God   Matthew 3:16 (see footnote)
- Is the Breath of God   John 20:21-23
- Spoke through the Old Testament kings, priests and prophets   Samuel 16:13, Luke 1:1-23,67 Ezekiel 2:1-2 (see footnote)
- Aointed Jesus for ministry   Luke 4:16-21
- Conceived Jesus in the womb of Mary   Matthew 1:18
- Descended like a dove upon Jesus at the Jordan River   Matthew 3:16-17
- Is the Spirit of God   Matthew 3:16 (see footnote)
- His coming was predicted by Jesus   Acts 1:4-5
- Empowers the believer   Acts 1:4-8
- Is the Teacher   Luke 12:12
- Is the Spirit of Truth and Guide to Truth   John 16:13-15
- Is the Counselor   John 14:15-16
- Was present at creation   Genesis 1:2
- Appeared as wind   Acts 2:2-3
- Appeared as tongues of fire   Acts 2:1-4
- Manifests gifts in the believer   1 Corinthians 12:1-11
- Can be grieved   Ephesians 4:29-30
- Is the promised gift   Acts 2:14-18
- Is our overflowing hope   Romans 15:13
- Brings the gift of prophesy   Joel 2:28
- Speaks in dreams and visions   Joel 2:28
- Enables men to speak with other tongues   Acts 2:1-4
- Is a gift to the Jew and the Gentile believer   Acts 15:6-9
- Does not speak on His own - only what He hears from Jesus   John 16:12-13
- Is the promise for Christians and their children   Acts 2:38-39
- Enables the believer to speak with boldness   Acts 4:31
- Exhibits fruit through the believer   Galatians 5:22-25
- Is given to the church to produce signs, wonders, miracles, healing, deliverance, conviction of sin, and release preaching   The Book of Acts

ANGELS

Angels are supernatural beings created by God. They move freely between heaven and earth. They exist in the same supernatural realm as God. These power-filled beings of light are God's assistants (Colossians 1:16) in the battle to establish His Kingdom. Their role in God's Kingdom is to serve and minister to God and to safeguard and minister to His people (Hebrews 1:7). They can appear in human form to assist people (Genesis 19:1), but are not to be worshipped. They actively participate with man in the battle to establish God's Kingdom.

ANGELIC FUNCTIONS

Angels Worship (Revelation 4:6-8)
Angels worship at the throne of God.

Angels Deliver Knowledge (Matthew 1:20, Luke 1:6)
Gabriel is the highest-ranking Messenger Angel. Gabriel also interperates visions/gives insight (Daniel 8:15, 9:21-23).

Angels Minister (Hebrews 1:14, Acts 12:7-10)
Angels are ministering spirits sent to serve those who will inherit salvation.

Angels Battle over Territories (Daniel 10:12-13)
Michael is the highest-ranking Warrior Angel. He is the Great Prince that protects the people of God (Daniel 10:30. 12:1).

Angels Guard (Revelation 2:1, Psalm 91:11, Psalm 34:7)
Angels guard children, adults and churches.

God has prepared eternal fire for the devil and the fallen angels* (Matthew 25:41), but God's Word speaks often of the glorious role of angels on God's side. These angels are highly visible in the prophetic *Book of Revelation.* There are legions of them (Psalm 68:17 see footnote and Matthew 26:53)! The following Bible story poignantly reveals large numbers of angels in their role of guarding and protecting.

*Fallen Angels: One third of the angels created by God revolted and chose to leave the presence of God. They are referred to as: Satan, demonic forces, forces of darkness. They can appear as angels of light to deceive people into following a way other than the true way - Jesus. They cannot maintain authority over a Christian.

ANGELS, THE CHARIOTS OF FIRE

Time and time again Elisha, the man of God, warned the king of Israel to be on his guard against the king of Aram. Enraged, Aram summoned his officers and demanded of them, "Will you not tell me which of you is on the side of the king of Israel?"

"None of us, my Lord," said one officer, "but Elisha the prophet tells the king of Israel the very words you speak in your bedroom." So the king sent horses, chariots and a strong army force to the city of Dothan. They went by night and surrounded the city. When the servant of Elisha arose the following morning he was stunned by the surrounding horses and chariots of war.

"Oh my lord, what shall we do?" The servant asked Elisha.

"Do not be afraid," the prophet answered. "Those who are with us are more than those who are with them." And, Elisha prayed, "Oh Lord, open the eyes of my servant so he may see!"

Then the Lord opened the servant's eyes. He looked and saw the hills full of horses and chariots of fire all around Elisha (2 Kings 6:16-25).

Angels supernaturally guarded Elisha. God has assigned to all His people these powerful, unseen warriors (angelic forces).

ETERNITY

Eternity is that state of existence prepared for us by the Father. It is an actual, glorious, everlasting place where man steps out of time and steps into living eternally, joyfully, permanently and supernaturally in the presence of God. This section reviews those areas of God's Kingdom dealing specifically with eternity.

THE CROSS

The Cross, the pivotal point of all history, is the most important symbol of God's Kingdom and of eternity. It is the victory upon which the entire Kingdom rests. Jesus was crucified and His blood shed to forgive our sins. The work of the Cross opens the door for the believer to enter eternal life. Jesus died and rose again. His death and resurrection prepares a way so that when we die we can rise again to eternal life.

ETERNAL LIFE

When you accept Jesus as Lord and Savior, you receive this free gift of eternal life. At that instant you enter into eternal life, you step into true reality. Eternal life is a free gift, paid for by the blood of Jesus. On the Cross Jesus erased for man the penalty of sin. Jesus has spoken:

"I am the resurrection and the life. He who believes in Me will live, even though he dies; and whosoever lives and believes in Me will never die (John 11:25)."

DEATH

What then is physical death if we are to live eternally? The physical body will die. At death, the person's soul and spirit enter into heaven, where they receive a new body - one that never dies. This is the entrance into everlasting life. Those left behind on earth experience sorrow because of the resulting separation. They can however, look forward with tremendous joy when they are reunited with loved ones in heaven for eternity. Death loses its grip when man becomes an eternal creature.

Where, oh Death, is your victory? Where, oh Death, is your sting? 1 Corinthians 15:55

THE LAMB'S BOOK OF LIFE

How does God know if a person is to receive eternal life? God keeps a record in heaven containing the names of those who have chosen Jesus as their Savior (Revelation 21:27). This record is called *The Lamb's Book of Life*.

Whenever anyone has their name in *The Lamb's Book of Life*, their sin has been paid for with the blood of Jesus and they can enter into the Kingdom of Heaven when their physical body dies. At that point they become part of the great cloud of witnesses who cheer for those still living on earth as we persevere and run the race marked out for us (Hebrews 12:1).

If a person's name is not in *The Lamb's Book of Life*, their own sin condemns them to eternal separation from God, in the lake of fire - a place of everlasting torment (Revelation 20:11-15).

PRAYER

Prayer is that eternal conversation between God and man about His Kingdom. It is making substance of God's Kingdom here on earth.

Prayer can take on many forms, such as requesting forgiveness, blessing, protection, healing, personal needs or intercession for friends, cities and nations. You can pray the prayer of faith, a prayer of thanksgiving, or a prayer of praise. Prayer can be loud. Prayer can be soft. You can be on your knees or you can be walking around a grocery store. Prayer is an on-going, honest conversation with God that builds relationship and friendship. For prayer, communing with God, is the substance of good relationship. Prayer is such an integral part of God's Kingdom experience it is as the air one breathes. Jesus gave us the Lord's Prayer as a model to teach us how to pray (Matthew 6:9-13).

Psalms 32:6 challenges: Let everyone who is godly pray. Ephesians 6:18 exhorts: Pray in the Spirit continually.

THE LORD'S PRAYER
Our Father in heaven, hallowed be Your name.
Your Kingdom come, Your will be done
On earth as it is in heaven.
Give us this day our daily bread.
Forgive our debts as we also have forgiven our debtors.
And lead us not into temptation,
But deliver us from the evil one.

HEAVEN

Here on earth, your physical body just wears out. But God offers eternity to man with the best retirement plan ever in an astounding place called heaven. And it is free!

Heaven is the eternal, holy dwelling place of God (Deuteronomy 26:15), the Creator of Heaven and Earth (Genesis 1:1, 14:19). God bestows citizenship in heaven (Philippians 3:20) and prepares a place for the Saints of God (those whose names are written in *The Lamb's Book of Life*). Here, the believer dwells forever in God's presence.

There are the heavens around the earth, the heavens of the universe, and the heaven where God has His throne - His holy dwelling place (Deuteronomy 16:15). God created them all. He is a God of immense creativity. Here on earth we have been able to admire some of His handiwork.

The Word of God only hints and gives occasional intriguing glimpse of this most splendid place. We know that the heaven where God rests upon His sapphire throne is surrounded by a rainbow (Ezekiel 1:26, 28). Angelic beings worship around this throne and so do men (Revelation 4:1-4, 9-11). This is where we will meet God face-to-face and worship Him.

The Word of God has given us some scriptural clues to aid in our concept of what heaven will be like. God made animals and the animals He made He called good. He tells us specifically there are animals in heaven. Revelation 19:11 purposely mentions horses. There are plants as *The Book of Revelation* also reveals trees of life that bear fruit, coming down from the throne of God (Revelation 21:2). Out of His throne also proceeds a great crystal river (Revelation 22:1). God has made every beautiful stone known to man - twelve-foot pearls on His heavenly gates, and gold to pave His streets (Revelation 22:2). So, there is a beautiful city in heaven (Revelation 21:2).

There we will be given a new, indestructible body and see our friends, family and those who have gone before us in the faith, including Old Testament prophets. God will wipe away our tears (Revelation 21:4) and give us a place of everlasting citizenship (Philippians 3:20). This place, prepared for us by God, is free. It is a place of eternal joy dwelling in the presence of God forever and ever!

THE RETURN OF THE KING

Before Jesus left His disciples almost 2,000 years ago, He told them that it was not for them to know the times and the dates the Father had set for His return (Acts 1:7). Right after Jesus returned to heaven two angels spoke to the disciples. The angels encouraged them saying Jesus would return the same way they saw Him go (Acts 1:10). No one knows about that day or hour, not even the angels in heaven. Only God the Father knows (Mark 13:32).

We know we live in a time close to the return of Jesus because of the prophetic signs around us. One very large prophetic signpost is the establishment of the Jewish state of Israel in 1948. Israel had not been a state for almost 2000 years. According to Biblical prophesy the state of Israel would once again be established and King Solomon's Temple will be rebuilt before Jesus will return. The time of the return of Jesus will be a time of great turmoil and strife for people, kingdoms and the heavens (Mark 13:5-37).

In Israel, in the city of Jerusalem, the Dome of the Rock, a Moslem temple sits squarely where King Solomon's Temple is reputed to be buried. There is a movement in the Holy Land to rebuild King Solomon's Temple. To build this temple, the Dome of the Rock might have to go. The Moslems, who currently occupy the Dome of the Rock, are most single-mindedly determined to stay in possession of this property.

When Jesus returns He will be coming back for His church, a church (His Bride) that is pure and holy and ready to receive Him (Revelation 19:7). When we see the Church of God pure and ready to receive Him and the temple rebuilt in Jerusalem we will know the return of Jesus is near!

At that time men will see the Son of Man coming in clouds with great power and glory, And He will send His angels and gather His elect from the four winds, from the ends of the earth to the ends of the heavens (Mark 13:26)

In the meantime, the focus is not to be the day and time of His return. The focus is to live our lives so that when Jesus does return we are found faithful.

REVIEW AND PROJECT

God is a triune God: Father, Son and Holy Spirit. At the same time He exists as one God. This God offers mankind the opportunity to choose to live in and understand the supernatural, eternal Kingdom of Heaven. This understanding begins through personally knowing His Son, the King of Kings, Jesus.

3
The True and Faithful King

God so loved the world that He gave His one and only Son that whoever believes in Him shall not perish but have eternal life. For God did not send His Son into the world to condemn the world, but to save the world through Him (John 3:16-17).

Jesus, the only Son of God, was conceived of the Holy Spirit, born of a virgin and became man so that He could bear the sin of the world. Between the ages of birth and thirty years of age we know little concerning His life. At the age of thirty He was baptized in the River Jordan by John the Baptist. In the Jordan River the Holy Spirit descended upon Jesus and His ministry began with signs and wonders following: preaching, healing the sick, raising the dead and casting out demons. At the age of thirty-three, Jesus was crucified. On the third day He rose from the dead and now reigns as our King of Kings and Lord of Lords. The story of His life is found in the four Gospels (meaning good news): *Matthew, Mark, Luke and John.*

JESUS

Jesus came in the flesh (2 John 7) and accepted the punishment due mankind cancelling the debt owed for sin that we could not pay. He became the curse to redeem us from sin and darkness. He is the Word of God that makes a contract with us and signs it in His sinless blood. For our benefit He disarms the powers and authorities triumphing over them by the Cross (Colossians 2:14-15).

Jesus, offers you His Kingdom along with all Kingdom benefits, including eternal life. If you do not choose God's Kingdom of Light, you automatically select to stay in the kingdom of darkness with all its negative benefits: death and destruction. Jesus sends forth this Kingdom Invitation to all the world:

Come to Me all who are weary and burdened and I will give you rest. Take My yoke upon you and learn from Me, for I am gentle and humble in heart and you will find rest for your souls (Matthew 11:28).
I am the Light of the World. Whoever follows Me will never walk in darkness but will have the light of life (John 8:12).

THE INVITATION

> **THE PRAYER OF SALVATION**
> Jesus, I am a sinner and I am lost without you. I ask you to forgive my sin. Come live in my heart and be my Lord and Savior. Amen

It is not the prayer that saves you but rather believing in your heart and confessing with your mouth that Jesus is your Lord. It is then you step out of a kingdom of darkness and into the Kingdom of Light. Your name is written in *The Lamb's Book of Life,* and you receive the free gift of eternal life. This experience is referred to as salvation - the state of acceptance of Jesus as the One who saves. From now on, you have an advocate with God the Father. You can confess and repent of your sin immediately to receive forgiveness and restore relationship.

If we are forgiven do we then continue to sin? No! While we no longer need to be slaves to sin (Romans 6), we must always accept responsibility for and confess our sin. God is faithful to forgive.

To deny we sin, or to pass the blame on to others for our sin is rebellion. Rebellion is the sin of witchcraft (1 Samuel 15:12-24 see footnote on verses 15, 23 and 24).

THE WORD OF GOD

In the beginning was the Word. The Word was with God and the Word was God. He was with God in the beginning (John 1:1-2) .

John's Gospel describes Jesus as the Word in John 1:1-2. The Bible is the living Word written down for all to read. This Word came to pass in the man-Jesus. The Bible is the source for learning about God and our relationship to Him. All that God the Father, God the Son and God the Holy Spirit ever speak will always agree with the Bible. Knowing God through His Word becomes a checkpoint for our own words, visions, dreams, ideas and directions. Scripture is anointed, God-breathed, and written under Holy Spirit inspiration (2 Timothy 3:16; 2 Peter 1:21).

Learning the ways and words of God needs to be under the direct supervision of the Holy Spirit. The Holy Spirit inspired all the Scripture, so He is the one who is to interpret it! He is the teacher - the only guide to all truth. Education with our own minds or own wisdom may lead us to know theology, but it does not lead us to know God.

As part of the study of the Word of God, the following areas will be reviewed: the four Gospels, how God's Word is a living Word, the difference between logos and rhema, why we should memorize God's Word and how to read His Word.

THE FOUR GOSPELS

The Book of Ezekiel speaks of the cherubim - the throne attendants. They are the four, living creatures who stand before the throne of God day and night shouting, *"Holy! Holy! Holy! Holy! Holy!"*

Each of the four has the face of a man, and on the right side each has the face of a lion and on the left side the face of an ox. Each also has the face of an eagle (Ezekiel 1:4-12). The man, the lion, the ox and the eagle are the symbols of the four Gospels. The four Gospels are not only written for us to read, but are so alive they stand before God's throne and shout! They are living attendants to the throne of God. Day and night they shout unto God, *"Holy! Holy! Holy! Holy!"*

The Gospels are the living story of the life and teachings of Jesus.

THE WORD OF GOD

The Bible stands as a book entirely different from all others. The Bible is a spiritual book not understood by carnal man. This book can only be understood by people who have the Spirit of God residing in them. Then the book opens and the Scriptures speak. Scriptures are written as a living word from a living God. Scriptures are not only living but they are truth (John 17:17). They are not only words that live but words to live by and words that live forever (1 Peter 1:25).

Scripture gives us a historical account of the struggles and travels of God's chosen people, an understanding of the relationship between God and His people, and personal comfort and support for one another via deliverance, healing, wisdom and discipline. Scriptures also teach and reveal coming events, and speak life into our future.

Other texts are either based upon mankind's "wisdom," contain true stories of lives past, are fictitious, or are from the fields of science, medicine or technology. No book is a living word unless it is written under the direct unction of the Holy Spirit and in full agreement with the Scriptures.

LOGOS AND RHEMA

In the Bible there are two types of living words. One is the actual written word on the page, logos. *Logos* can be read for wisdom, reference, historical perspective or insights into the relationship between God and His people.

The second type of living Word is called rhema. When a specific Scripture leaps out and you know God is speaking directly to you, you just read a rhema word from God. Rhema words are the divine utterances of God.

Discernment helps you recognize if a message is a Word of God for education or a Word of God for you right now. If you act upon the Word as if it is a rhema word, and it really was a logos word, you can be in for a fall.

Remember when Jesus invites Peter to walk on the water (Matthew 14:29)? What if one reads that Word and they think they should have the power to walk on water? Unless God had spoken directly to them in a rhema word they would drown or at least appear quite foolish. Differentiate between logos and rhema for yourself. Ask God and seek His confirmation!

God is faithful to confirm His Word to us. He will confirm in several different ways. It is His desire to develop this conversation/ relationship with His chosen people.

This relationship is a continually, developing process whereby we open ourselves and make ourselves available to God. We talk to Him, listen for His answers and read His Word. He responds to us. We have conversation. We gain understanding. We recognize His voice.

HIDE THE WORD IN YOUR HEART

I have hidden your Word in my heart that I might not sin against You. Psalm 119:11

Memorizing Scripture from the Bible helps change wrong patterns of thinking. If you know the real Word and the real God, you will not be easily swayed to accept counterfeits. Memorizing takes the Word of God and works it into your physical reactions and into the thoughts of your heart.

Hiding the Word of God in your heart allows you to tear down the kingdom of the world that is natural to your thoughts and build a response to the Kingdom of God. When you need to take action you can respond with Kingdom thinking and therefore, reap Kingdom benefits.

Memorization tears down worldly structures and assists in building on a strong Kingdom foundation. Kingdom thinking is not just head thinking. Kingdom thinking is heart thinking. Perhaps you have not considered that you think with your heart, but the Word tells us that as a man thinks in his heart, so he is (Proverbs 23:7, Matthew 15:9, Proverbs 16:9). Memorizing is hiding the Word of God deep in your heart so that your heart knows and will give forth Kingdom thinking when you come to difficult circumstances.

Retrain your heart. Invite the Holy Spirit to guide your studies. Pray that the eyes of your heart will open so you can truly see.

READING THE LIVING WORD

There are different approaches to reading the Scriptures. Some people find passages and "chew" on them, devouring and understanding one small portion at a time. Some memorize section after section, while others read several books to get the overview.

Different personality types can approach God's Word from different perspectives. Insisting that everyone learn the same way ignores the fact that we were created uniquely and have different views to lend to the body of Christ. While one view is not better than another, we will tend to gravitate more towards one type of learning than another because of our personality type or because of the season of life in which God has us walking. Different perspectives allow balance and variety and reveal different aspects of God.

THE CONTRACT SIGNED IN BLOOD

The Bible is divided into two sections: The Old and New Testaments. This division is also known as the Old and the New Covenants. These covenants explain the contract God has with His Kingdom people.

Under the Old Covenant, the sins of the Jewish people were covered through the blood sacrifice of an unblemished lamb and by following the Law. Under the New Covenant, the blood covering for the forgiveness of sin is the Blood of Jesus and is a covenant of grace. Jesus is the Lamb, sacrificed once and for all. Jesus is our advocate with God the Father. Through Him, the relationship with God the Father that was lost at the fall of man is restored.

When we as Gentile believers (non-Jews) are grafted into the promises of the Old Covenant, we become as children of Abraham -the children of faith (Ephesians 2:11-13). God calls us His chosen people, a royal priesthood and the people of God, just as He calls the Jewish people His chosen people (1 Peter 2:9). We become the friends of God (John 15:14-15). Because Jesus has paid the price for our sin, when God looks at us He sees the blood that has paid the redemption price and we are righteous in His sight.

Two thousand years ago, Jesus, Son of God, born of a virgin, became man and restored our relationship. Each and every citizen of God's Kingdom chooses to become a citizen and come under this Blood Covenant. Until that choice is made, man's nature is not renewed and His nature turns toward sin. Man's true nature lies along the path of hostility towards God (Romans 8:5-7). But through Jesus and His Blood offering, we become more than conquerors (Romans 8:28-39). Because of this covenant nothing can separate us from His all consuming love, for His covenants are everlasting.

Salvation demands nothing but acceptance, not good works! Salvation stands as finished and completely paid for by the Blood of Jesus in the perfect sacrifice Jesus offered on the Cross.

This sacrifice purchases certain rights and privileges for those under the New Covenant. These rights and privileges enable Kingdom citizens to be co-heirs with Jesus. We are given the right to rule and reign with Jesus (Revelation 5:10 and II Timothy 2:12).

As we enter this covenant with Jesus, all that Jesus has, becomes ours. Simultaneously, all we consider belonging to us, becomes His.

POWER IN THE BLOOD

This Covenant is a binding contract (solemn agreement, legal document) between God and man. It is through this Blood of Jesus (in the New Testament) that our relationship (as Gentile believers) with the God is established.

In the Old Testament, because of the blood covenant of the lamb, the Hebrews were under God's protection. As they faithfully kept the conditions of the covenant, they were successful in battle and protected from disease, plagues and from their enemies.

In Exodus 12:21-23, Moses directs the children of Israel to place the slaughtered blood of an unblemished lamb on the top and both sides of the door frames of their homes. At midnight the Lord passes over the homes of the Egyptians and the homes of the Hebrews. Judgment comes to the Egyptian homes without the blood upon the door frames; however, all under the blood are protected. The Israelites remember and still celebrate this day yearly as the Day of Passover, because the Lord passed over and did not permit the Destroyer to enter the houses marked with the blood of the lamb.

THE CUP OF FRIENDSHIP

Jesus took bread, gave thanks and broke it, and gave it to them saying, "This is My body given for you; do this in remembrance of Me." Then Jesus took the cup saying, "This cup is the New Covenant in My Blood, which is poured out for you." Luke 22:19-20

Before Jesus was crucified, He reclined at a table to share the Passover Feast with twelve of His friends (disciples). Here Jesus establishes the New Covenant in His blood - the Blood of the Lamb of God. Jesus was willing to pay a staggering price to offer this cup of friendship. He sacrificed Himself so that we may be under His protection. He gave His Blood so that the Destroyer has to pass over and may not destroy those under the covering of His friendship. The power is in the Blood that was shed - the Blood that establishes the New Covenant. Every time we partake in sharing this supper Jesus established, we embrace in covenant with Him. We claim this covenant for ourselves and for our family. Before taking actual communion we need to spend time to examine ourselves and confess sin.

> **PASSOVER PRAYER**
> In the name of Jesus I declare that the blood of Jesus, the Lamb of God, is upon the doorposts of my house. The Destroyer must pass over and may not destroy the family under the covering of the blood of Jesus!

THE SEAL OF THE KING

Having believed you were marked in Him with a seal, the promised Holy Spirit who is a deposit guaranteeing your inheritance (Ephesians 1:13b - 14a). God seals us as His very own. He places a seal upon our heart. The Holy Spirit is that seal...the King's stamp upon your heart that you belong to Him.

THE WILL OF THE KING

KNOW that all things, God has the power to do what He has promised (Romans 4:21).

KNOW that you are not your own, but have been purchased with a price (1 Corinthians 6:20).

KNOW that God has a plan and purpose for your life (Jeremiah 29:11). *"For I know the plans I have for you," declares the Lord, "plans to prosper you, and not to harm you, plans to give you hope and a future."*

REVIEW AND PROJECT

Jesus, the only Son of God, chose to become man. He was completely like us in everything except sin. Because He was a blameless man before God, He could offer His Blood as a sacrifice for sinful man. When you receive Jesus into your heart, you appropriate that perfect sacrifice and by faith step out of the kingdom of darkness into God's Kingdom of Light. At that point your name is written in a book in heaven called *The Lamb's Book of Life*, and you receive the gift of eternal life. So begins the New Covenant relationship. This Covenant is a binding contract. We actively participate in and call to mind our covenant through sharing the Lord's Supper, also called communion.

The next chapter deals with how to maintain a holy relationship through repenting and receiving God's mercy and grace. It also continues to develop our foundational relationship through water baptism and the Baptism of the Holy Spirit.

4
Prepare for the Kingdom

In the Old Testament, the Glory of God dwelt in tents as His people moved from place to place. When the Israelites finally entered the Promised Land, they desired to build a permanent temple for God where the Ark of the Covenant could rest and the Glory of the Lord would reside.

In the New Testament, His dwelling place is in every Christian. We offer our bodies to be His holy temple. We repent and turn from those things which grieve God's heart so that we may offer Him a holy dwelling place, a sacred temple, a dwelling dedicated totally to Him (1 Corinthians 3:16). We prepare our hearts to fully receive God's Kingom.

Part of this preparation is through the confession of sin. The following is simply a good reference check to expose areas where the enemy might have a foothold in your life. It is also a good reference check for those who are ready to experience the Baptism of the Holy Spirit. When you experience the Baptism of the Holy Spirit, you open yourself to view and become more sensitive to the spiritual world. Areas of deception not cleared out can lead to spiritual confusion and further deception. (Baptism of the Holy Spirit is discussed on pages 31-33.)

REPENT

The list on the next page contains suggestions of areas that may need attention. First, you repent of the sin (express genuine sorrow) and ask God for forgiveness. Check these areas so you may wisely reject the ways of your enemy, Satan, and fully embrace God's Kingdom. With every sin forgiven, you acquire the provision to deal with issues in appropriate, godly ways.

A door can be opened into a person's spirit and soul through sinful, careless, personal decisions. Foolish decisions can be terribly costly. The enemy then has an invitation to enter and deceive until he is confronted and evicted.

How do you expel this unwelcome tenant? First, you name the sin and ask God for forgiveness. Next, in the name of Jesus you command that influence to go out the door through which it arrived. Pray that the opening be closed and the Cross of Jesus bar the enemy from returning. Repent of the sin, cast out the deceiver and then invite God to fill the area with His Holy Spirit. We seize the freedom the Kingdom offers through repenting and confession sin.

Review the following list for possible ways you may have come under mind control, accepted philosophies or attempted to seek guidance for your life in ways contrary to God's Word (see Deuteronomy 18:9:14, Leviticus 19:26-32, Revelation 21:6-8).

- Lying and other specific personal sin
- Spirit Guides/Voodo Hexes
- Dungeons and Dragons or Games linked to Witchcraft/Occult
- Mind control, ESP
- Clairvoyance
- Séances (consulting the dead)
- Levitation, Transcendental Meditation
- Water Witching
- Drugs
- Fortune Telling, Horoscope Guidance, Palm Reading, Tea Leaves
- Racism
- Astral Projection, Telekinesis
- Humanistic Philosophy
- Ouja Boards
- Cults, Religious Legalism, Religious (not godly) life-style
- *Karate, Martial Arts, Yoga
- Eastern, Asian Religions, Meditations or New Age practices
- Pornography
- Sexual Activity/Affairs, Deviant Sexual Behavior**
- Witchcraft or other Satanic Practices
- Rebellion
- Abortion or Assisted Suicide

*Objects such as the following, or activities mentioned above
Ankhs, Buddha's/Idols
Good - Luck Charms, Greek Gods/Goddesses/Mermaids
"Healing" Crystals
Witchcraft Symbols, Horoscope Signs, Egyptian Crosses
Pegasus/Fairies/Unicorns
Indian Medicine Bags or any objects associated with Voodoo

We are to be a holy people, set apart to God. Therefore, you reject those things God considers unholy: areas where you seek revelation in any way other than through Him, or those areas in which you rebel against Him. He considers those areas an abomination and witchcraft, just as He did in the Old Testament. Just like His people in the Old Testament, He will discipline you.

This does not mean that everything listed above is all bad. There are some good ideas, neat concepts, stirring sayings and high-sounding intentions promoted by well-meaning and nice people. But God is a jealous God (Exodus 20:4-6). He desires that you learn from Him, practice His ways and have a heart that excludes all other philosophies and ways of worship.

You not only offend God's holy nature, but when you accept something not of Him, you are more prone to justifying further involvement - involvement that can lead you away from an intimate relationship with God. Walk carefully, for Hollywood will sugarcoat white witchcraft, that is, using witchcraft for seemingly harmless or moralistic purposes. Many, even famous Christians, may justify it as good because it represents doing good with good people.

*Pagan worship, superstition, eastern religions, meditations or philosophies can train the mind in methods of thinking contrary to Scripture and open doors of deception in the mind and heart. Some actions can be actual acts of praise to an oriental god. Check carefully and understand fully what you are doing. You could be fully ignorant of what is transpiring and yet, at the same time be participating in a type of religious worship.

** Read Romans 1:24-32. Be cautious what the eyes see, the ears hear and the heart receives as truth. A diet of television programs, movies, music and soap operas that promote an interest and acceptance of easy sex is hazardous to your spiritual health. Cartoons that glorify and promote interest in the occult and eastern philosophy are hazardous to the health of your children.

Any form or use of witchcraft for any reason is strictly forbidden by God! There are no exceptions! It involves the supernatural, not of God, and opens your spirit to serious deception. If you are presently involved in any of these areas, or have been in the past, you may have become exposed to spiritual deception and future problems effecting your mind, will and emotions. Praying the following prayer, as well as listening and watching for the Holy Spirit's discernment, helps you gain freedom. To remain free, make the commitment to stay away from these influences and to remove any influences from your home environment.

If you fall in one of these areas again, just repeat this prayer with a friend. If you still need help, seek counseling, Inner Healing or Deliverance. Personal repentance is an area to revisit often in prayer.

THE PRAYER TO REPENT: Personal

Lord, I confess my involvement in _____ (area of sin).
Forgive me for seeking revelation in any way than through You!
Please continue to reveal any area in my heart where I have hidden sin, rebellion or witchcraft. Now, in the Name of Jesus,
I command deception or any influence not of Jesus, that entered my life as a result of a foolish choice, to leave through the opening where you entered. In the Name of Jesus, I close the door and bar the opening with the Cross of Jesus. I invite the Holy Spirit to come and fill this place in my heart and my life. Amen!

GENERATIONAL FORGIVENESS

The Cross not only has the power to overcome the influence of past indiscretions, it also has the power to stop family curses. Sins can follow a family line through several generations. Sometimes even illnesses can follow through family generations.

Family (generational) curses are hindrances, negative patterns of behavior or sometimes illnesses that follow through generations in a family. Your grandfather could have opened a doorway to deception that allowed a negative influence to enter the family line, paving the way for evil to take hold - literally opening a portal to the supernatural world for evil to enter. These influences can then follow and torment the family to the fourth generation (Exodus 20:5). Some families become so accustomed to a particular influence that they think of it as normal.

For a variety of reasons, not everything immediately responds to this type of prayer. However, the search can prove to be very valuable and freeing! You can ask for forgiveness for the trespasses and rebellion of your relatives, and that the rebellion and sin they passed down to you through their choices will be forgiven. You can also pray that any evil heritage will have to change to blessing.

Forgive the evil handed down to you in the form of words spoken over you or choices family members made. Realize it was the enemy at work trying to destroy you. You could draw a chart noting specific sins with specific parents and grandparents. Then, repent for each individual iniquity and transgression that is part of your inheritance. This may need further prayer, particulary if you do not experience complete freedom. Deliverance is covered in *The Power - Christian Primary III.*

As you study a family list always keep a balance. Curses follow to the fourth generation but blessings in a family follows a family line through the throusandth generation. So, you also have many family blessings. Know too, Jesus broke all these curses for you as He hung upon the cross. Now choose to appropriate this gift of freedom that has already been given for you.

- Divorce
- Mental Illness/Nervous Breakdowns
- Murder
- Suicide
- Abortion
- Intellectualism
- Jealousy
- Sexual sin
- Rebellious Nature
- Disabilities
- Alcohol and/or Drug Abuse
- Witchcraft, Wicca, (White Witchcraft, Witchcraft done for supposedly good)
- Some Genetic Hearing Loss/Genetic Color Blindness
- Constant Debt
- Physical Illnesses
- A Critical Spirit
- Abusive Behaviors/Manipulation

ORGANIZATIONS: Masons, Job's Daughters, all cults
ABUSE: Sexual, physical, suicide, thoughts of suicide

Anything from the personal list above can be included in prayer. Also a person's nationality could possibility influence their decisions. Praying and placing the Cross between a person's home country and themselves and praying that all not pleasing to Jesus stop at the Cross (all positive influences to continue) is one more way to pray. You can also repent of sin for your nationality. You can also stand and forgive those who have persecuted your nationality. Jesus has already made provisions to acquire these freedoms for us, now we just lay claim to our rightful inheritance (Isaiah 53:1-12).

PRAYER TO REPENT: Family

Dear Jesus, I confess the sin of _____ (name the sin) in my family. I repent for the sin and ask You to forgive this sin in my family. Stop the power of this generational curse. I place the Cross between my father and mother and their families four generations back and command this sin, or curse, which has followed my family through the generations to stop at the Cross. This iniquity is no longer my inheritance, the inheritance of my family, nor the inheritance of my children. But rather I receive blessing to a thousandth generation.
(Leviticus 26:40-42, Deuteronomy 7:9, Exodus 20:4-6)

GRACE AND MERCY

We can repent over the past in choosing to close out of our lives negative influences, and we can confront generational sins of our families. But there are just times we need to repent over present issues of sin - that ball and chain that holds us captive. To repent means: spending quality time before God and unabashedly pleading for His grace and His mercy. There is genuine sorrow for sin and an active pursuit of forgiveness. Judgment is what we deserve! But, when we reach out to God He is gracious and full of mercy.

Grace is God's favor - His unmidigated pardon. Through His grace He forgives a repentant heart. He willingly gives His grace to the humble (Proverbs 3:34).

Not only does God abound in grace towards us, He also offers

His great mercy (Proverbs 5:17, II Samuel 24:14). And when we cried to Him for His mercy He will hear our cry (Psalms 28:6).

To feel sorrow for our sin is a prayer of humility - a prayer composed by the heart crying out for the mercy and the grace only God can give. We pray this prayer for the sin that we cannot overcome on our own.

This kind of prayer is not a formal written prayer. It is through tears of repentance that mercy and grace are obtained. It is only through humbling ourselves and seeking His grace and His mercy that we receive this profound gift.

BE BAPTIZED

Peter challenges the early Church, "Repent and be Baptized!" Both Peter and John the Baptist speak of two baptisms (Matthew 3:1, Acts 2: 38,39). The first baptism, washes away sin. Man becomes a new creature, dead to sin and alive to Christ (John 1:4). The second baptism is with the Holy Spirit and fire (Acts 1:4; Matthew 3:11) with signs following (Mark 16:15-16, Acts 22:16) as in *The Book of Acts*.

Jesus experiences both baptisms. Of Jesus' first thirty years, we know little. But, the moment He is baptized in water and receives the Holy Spirit, He initiates His battle with evil and launches His ministry, with signs and wonders following (Matthew 3:16-17, Mark 1:9-13).

John the Baptist preaches water baptism. But the ministry of the New Testament Church begins only after the disciples receive the second baptism, the Baptism of the Holy Spirit. Both baptisms are an intregral part of the New Testament Church: water for the forgiveness of sin and the Baptism of the Holy Spirit for the power to live the Christian experience. They are necessary acts of faith for the believer - one following another (Acts 2:1-17).

Those who have received Jesus as Lord and Savior already have received the Holy Spirit, because God exists as one, inseparable, triune God. When you receive Jesus into your heart, the Father and the Holy Spirit also come to abide.

When we receive Jesus He forgives all our sin. Yet, we still are to be baptized with water for the washing away of our sin. This baptism is a total immersion into Jesus, producing a new creature, dead to sin but alive in Christ.

We already have the Holy Spirit, but when we ask by faith to be baptized with the Holy Spirit and with fire, we come forth immersed in power to be a believer.

THE BAPTISM IN THE HOLY SPIRIT

John the Baptist declared that there was one coming after him whose sandals he was not fit to carry who would baptize with the Holy Spirit and with fire (Matthew 3:11).

Jesus declares, "I am going to send you what my Father has promised (Like 24:45-49)." Acts 1:5, Jesus directs His followers, "Do not leave Jerusalem, but wait for the gift my Father promised... For John baptized with water but in a few days you will be baptized with the Holy Spirit."

When the day of Pentecost came they were all together in one place. Suddenly a sound like the blowing of a violent wind came from heaven and filled the whole house where they were sitting. They saw what seemed to be tongues of fire that separated and came to rest on each of them. All of them were filled with the Holy Spirit and began to speak in other tongues as the Spirit enabled them, and signs and wonders followed (Acts 2:1-4).

The following is a prayer to be filled with the power of the Holy Spirit. Note that some churches have an actual event called confirmation where they pray f or the release of the Holy Spirit to an individual. At that point the Church has passed on this special relationship to the individual. The individual may have received the gift but never actually opened the gift they received from the Church. Either way, here is an opportunity to become personally acquainted with the third person of the Trinity - the Holy Spirit. The Holy Spirit is the one and only true guide to fully understanding God's Kingdom. The Holy Spirit is the only spirit guide to truth.

THE HOLY SPIRIT PRAYER
Father, thank you for sending Your Holy Spirit!
In the Name of Jesus I receive the Holy Spirit.
Thank You, Holy Spirit, that You are the Spirit of Truth and
that You will lead me into all truth (John 16:26, Mark 16:15-18).

Jesus asked the Father to send the promised Holy Spirit: We can ask on our own behalf, or ask someone who has had the experience to lay hands on us to release this gift to us (Acts 19:1-6).

<u>The First Sign:</u> The first sign to follow is speaking in other tongues. This is the same sign the first church experienced in Acts 2:1-4; 19:6. Speaking in tongues is choosing to open your mouth and making an effort to produce sounds. The Holy Spirit will take over your beginning babble and you will experience a brand-new language. It is a yielding and surrendering of your tongue to make sounds. This physical action of faith allows you to accept and receive the gift being offered.

<u>Expect:</u> Sometime between a few minutes to a few days following your initial experience, you can anticipate your eyes to open to spiritual truths you could not understand before. In addition, a great flood of joy or emotions and an intensive learning experience often occurs. As you seek the relationship the gifts of the Spirit will follow.

<u>Revelation and Power:</u> The Holy Spirit reveals Jesus and the Father. Now you have received the revelation and Holy Spirit power to live successfully God's Kingdom experience (Mark 16:15-18, Matthew 28:18-20)! This power is like releasing dynamite into your life. The word actually used in *The Book of Acts*, "the power", of the Holy Spirit, means, "the dynamite" of the Holy Spirit.

<u>Signs and Wonders:</u> In the Old Testament, revelation was evidenced through a prophet, priest or king. Today, the revelation is experienced as you grow in your experience and relationship with the Holy Spirit. The Holy Spirit empowers you with gifts of signs and wonders as He did with new believers in *The Book of Acts*. God and His Word have not changed. In the last days the Holy Spirit will be poured out on all people (Joel 2:28-32).

The Holy Spirit becomes your teacher/counselor, the one who leads you into all truths. The Holy Spirit is so transparent that all He does is reveal Jesus. It is the Holy Spirit's responsibility to open your understanding to the Scriptures, to give you dreams and visions and to incorporate into your being the nine gifts of the Spirit and nine fruits of the Spirit.

The nine gifts of the Holy Spirit are messages of wisdom, messages of knowledge, faith, healing, miraculous powers, prophecy, distinguishing between spirits, giving a prophecy in tongues, interpretation of tongues. (1 Corinthians 12:8-11).

The nine fruits of the Spirit are: love, joy, peace, patience, kindness, goodness, faithfulness, gentleness and self-control (Galatians 5:22).

REVIEW AND PROJECT

This chapter reviews several ways to deal with sin, from repenting of negative influences, to stopping family curses and finally, to simply crying our for the grace and mercy of God. We deserve judgement, but God offers His grace and mercy to those who truly and humbly seek it.

Now that you have established a heart relationship (friendship) with Jesus, have participated in repentance, been immersed in baptism of water and received the gift of the Holy Spirit, you are ready to begin possessing God's Kingdom here on earth for yourseves and for others.

In the following chapters, are methods and approaches to godly choices. These choices are truly the foundation for Christian living. Do not expect to learn and to apply everything at once. It is a matter of realizing the availability and beginning a journey that will last a lifetime.

God's desire for your life is for you to progress into becoming a mature believer. His Kingdom offers a firm foundation for living successfully above and beyond all the world has to offer.

Love, faith and hope are the three standards of the Kingdom of Heaven. They are like beacons of light revealing the ancient pathway to God. Now step forth upon this ancient pathway into the very heart and soul of God's Kingdom.

5
The Kingdom Standards

To occupy God's Kingdom you must be persistent and be determined! Second Kings 13:13-19 recounts the story of the Prophet Elisha and, Jehoash, King of Israel. Elisha was suffering from the illness from which he would very soon die. King Jehoash recognized the prophet was of greater significance for Israel's military success than even Israel's military forces and so king Jehoash came to see Elisha for the last time before the great prophet died. Jehoash wanted the Lord's blessing however he lacked persistence and determination.

Elisha said to Jehoash, "Take the arrows," and the king took them. Elisha told him, "Strike the ground." The king struck it three times and stopped. The man of God was angry with the king and said, "You should have struck the ground five or six times; then you would have defeated Aram and completely destroyed it. But now you will defeat it only three times" (2 Kings 13:18-19).

The unenthusiastic response to Elisha's directive reflected insufficient zeal for accomplishing the task (footnote 2 Kings 13:19).

STRIKE THE GROUND

The king was advised to take his tools of war and strike the ground. But the king did it without perseverance and without zeal and so the king could be only moderately successful in his military campaigns.

What was the purpose of the prophet asking the king to strike the ground? In the beginning, all of the ground belonged to God and reflected His glory. But at the fall of Adam, the ground came under a curse (Genesis 3:17-19). The ground was now where the snake crawled upon its belly (Genesis 3:14).

To restore the ground back to its rightful ownership the king had to beat it with his tools of warfare in a supernatural act of faith before he could claim it in the natural. In faith he was to strike the ground, beating back the curse of fear, doubt and the lies of the snake. By relying on the supernatural (the Holy Spirit direction as given by the Prophet) he could then reclaim the land once more in the natural.

Under the New Covenant we do not choose arrows as our tools of warfare. Jesus revealed to us the way to devastate the power of the enemy and restore His Kingdom. He opened the door for His Kingdom to be restored through His example of perfect forgiveness and perfect love. The key is perservance and determination.

With the Holy Spirit as your guide, use His supernatural tools to beat the land. These tools are love, faith and hope. Strike the ground by choosing God's Kingdom standards. Strike the ground until your actions bring forth the desired result in the natural. Persevere with the greatest of zeal in this supernatural action until the curses are broken and the victory is yours. You not only strike the ground, you beat the ground until the victory is won, for the Kingdom of Heaven is taken by violence and the violent take it by force.

LOVE - THE LAW OF THE KINGDOM

Love is the very heartbeat of the Kingdom. If we have not love we have not the Kingdom. Jesus laid down His life as the perfect blood sacrifice to completely cover the requirements of the Old Testament Law (as given to Moses in Exodus 20:1-17). In the New Testament we are under the law of mercy and grace, the Law of Love. Jesus restates The Old Testament Law in the Law of Love.

Love the Lord your God with all your heart and with all your soul and with all your mind. This is the first and greatest commandment. And the second is like it: Love your neighbor as yourself (Matthew 22:37-39).

Old Testament law though, still plays a role in the life of a believer - not as a measure of salvation but as a moral and ethical guide obeyed out of love for God. It is the Spirit that provides the power to love.(Romans 8:4-5).

Jesus turned the Old Covenant of Law into a New Covenant of Love. We obey now not out of obedience to fulfill the requirements of Law, but because of His love written upon our hearts. We live in relationship and know when we fail we can ask and obtain immediate forgiveness.

Jesus set us free under His Covenant of Love. It is a covenant of His mercy and His grace. Jesus loves us unconditionally, freeing us to choose to love others unconditionally and to forgive others unconditionally. When we listen and follow the Spirit, we are heirs of God and co-heirs with Christ (Romans 8:15-17). Love is a choice we can make as God's spirit of love dwells in us.

CHOOSE LOVE

Everyone has a free will. Our freedom is the most valuable gift we have been given. We must guard it zealously and use it wisely. This gift of freedom which God grants to mankind is nothing less than the freedom to choose.

We are not to give up our free will, nor lay it at the feet of another. Each one of us is accountable before God for the choices we make. We use our free will wisely when we make the Kingdom choice to love others and to obey God. Over the next few pages are examples to clarify how you can choose to love in all circumstances.

Love is a choice. You choose how you will act and how you will respond. Once you secure that Kingdom choice, your feelings follow. Jesus chooses to love us unconditionally, so we are free to choose to love others unconditionally. Jesus' covenant with us is one of love (John 15:9-12). Love is a choice of our free will.

You do not love sin but you love people, separating the sin from the person so you can love without condition. When you choose to love, Jesus' supernatural love flows through you. When you cannot love, Jesus' supernatural love will flow through you and change you. We will always come to the end of being able to love when love is based upon our own abilities. It is only Jesus in us and through us that can pour out as love.

God reveals true love is in the following declaration found in 1 Corinthians.

LOVE is patient, LOVE is kind,
It does not envy,
It does not boast,
It is not proud.
It is not rude,
It is not self-seeking,
It is not easily angered,
It keeps no record of wrongs.
LOVE does not delight in evil but rejoices with the truth.
It always protects,
Always trusts,
Always hopes,
Always perseveres.
LOVE never fails!
1 Corinthians 13:1-7

LOVE NEVER FAILS

Everyone has feelings. Feelings are not necessarily right or wrong. Feelings are temporary and can change from moment to moment. They can be fragile, fickle and deceptive. Feelings differ from love because love does not depend upon feelings. Feelings are to follow choices. This is a completely different pattern from that of the world. The world says, "You don't feel love? Then love is gone!" Kingdom love is based upon commitment and choice.

Sometimes you can feel as if you are not in love, or no longer can love, because you have been hurt. Your emotions and feelings, however, will follow the choices you make. You can, for instance, choose love. In choosing love, you choose to forgive, choose to be healed and choose to bless - feelings should not rule over these decisions. When you rule over your emotions, the power of God's Kingdom can be released to others. Since God's Kingdom is a Kingdom of Love, when you choose love you connect with the power that sets people free.

You are not to totally ignore feelings, for they can warn of danger, be a checkpoint in relationships, or a reminder to take care of your physical body. But you do not depend upon feelings for your relationship with God or with others.

HOW TO CHOOSE LOVE WHEN YOU HAVE BEEN HURT

There are both intentional and unintentional hurts: hurts that cause us to withdraw our love and become protective, angry, bitter, hateful or full of revenge. We build offenses (fences) and not only keep the person who offended us outside but we carry it over to new people or new situation and apply our standard there also. The fences we build surround us preventing us from being free, free to move into our future. But there is no moving when you are stuck inside a fence.

We will always experience hurt. Everyone experiences hurt. The reason for our hurt is not as important as how we respond to our hurt. If we have been hurt or feel we can no longer love others, we need to stand and forgive. Forgiveness is a three step process.

THE FIRST STEP IN FORGIVENESS

The first step is simple but profound: we must choose to forgive, as God commands (Colossians 3:12-14). When we stand to pray, forgive (Mark 11:25-26). We forgive so our sins might be forgiven, as Jesus taught us in *The Lord's Prayer* (Matthew 6:12-15). We forgive to release others and ourselves from darkness (John 20:23). We forgive because the Lord forgave - and forgives us. We forgive because God forgives those we forgive.

Forgiveness releases both the person forgiving and the one who needs forgiveness. Jesus set the greatest example when He spoke from the Cross and asked God the Father to forgive those who crucified Him declaring that they didn't know what they were doing (Luke 23:34). Jesus forgave. That was the power of His love.

Lack of forgiveness imprisons others and us. If we stand in judgment and do not forgive, we bind those who offended us, and we also end up in darkness ourselves (Matthew 18:21-35).

Forgiveness is not easy, but it is the only Kingdom choice. Sometimes we do not feel like forgiving, but since forgiveness is a choice of our will, choose forgiveness rather than feelings. Your feelings will follow your choices. You continue to choose until you own that choice.

You can always forgive, but that does not necessarily mean you should always trust. If you are in a situation where you or your children are being physically abused, neglected or forsaken, forgive but do not continue to stay. God will make a way. Ask Him and He will direct you.

THE SECOND STEP IN FORGIVENESS

The second step is to release the hurt. So often, this second part of forgiveness is completely forgotten, and the hurt continues to torment us, surfacing again in actions or reactions. When walls (offenses) within prevent us from loving again, it may be because hurts have not been completely resolved. Release your hurt, determining that it will not rule over you or your relationship(s). Ask Jesus to heal your hurt completely - allow Him to heal. Place your hand on your heart and speak healing to your heart! Healing can be instantaneous or take place over an extended time. Perservere until your healing is complete.

As people under the Covenant of Love, we must settle this issue in our hearts once and for all - our choice is love. To choose to love does not mean to choose to trust. Know the heart condition of others and realize some people are not worthy of trust.

THE THIRD STEP IN FORGIVENESS

Finally, we bless those who have spitefully used us - Christians and non - Christians. Non - Christians do not know God and really need forgiveness - God's and ours (Romans 12:14, Matthew 5:43- 48). When they come against us, they have touched the apple of God's eye. When thinking of them, bless them in their job, bless their children, bless their home, bless them in any and every way possible until the hurt has been forgotten. Blessing can not only be a prayer, but also an action. Bless these people with an act of kindness.

Think of your children, (even the errant ones) as well as spouses or relatives, and others, praying blessings into their lives. As long as you feel negative, pray blessings on and for them.

God wants you to learn and grow even if your hurt is not healed immediately. Continue to forgive, asking for healing and blessing every time the painful memory returns. Do this until the memory no longer hurts - not one minute longer, not one minute shorter. Keep striking that ground until you own it and you are free of the negative feelings.

Once, I prayed three years over an unpleasant memory. I do not know why it took so long (while other memories resolved more quickly), but I knew the process, and I persevered.

We cannot skip any steps in this process: forgiving, healing and blessing. All three are equally important.

> **FORGIVENESS PRAYER**
> In the Name of Jesus, I choose to forgive _____
> (name of person). I stand and forgive this person for
> _____(offense). I ask God to touch
> my heart right now and heal every hurt I have received from this
> person. I ask God to touch and heal them. I pray God will
> pour out these blessings on those who have hurt me:
> _____, _____,
> and _____ Amen.

WHEN YOU NEED TO BE FORGIVEN

Actively seek forgiveness if you are at fault. Do not allow pride to prevent the restoration of the relationship. Go to the person you have wronged and talk to them. Do not let them avoid the issue by saying, "That's ok." It is not ok to hurt others.

If you have approached the person you wronged with humility and sincerely offered apologies yet they refuse to forgive you, forgive them, pray for their healing and bless them. Very painful offenses may require a period of time for restoration to occur; a trust relationship may never be the same and a very precious friendship may be lost forever through carelessness. But be encouraged, as working through hurts most often binds people closer than they were before.

BE PREPARED

Relationships can be very difficult and can include intense feelings of anger. You may feel angry when someone is completely insensitive or invades your personal "space." Anger should not be stuffed inside and ignored (This kind of response can cause severe depression). Anger should be confronted and resolved. When you express anger, you should not display your temper in harmful ways. Shouting, name-calling or dragging up issues from the past only makes the problem more difficult to resolve. When dealing with anger, it is helpful to set some ground rules for yourself before problems surface. Think through how you will handle anger - your own anger, as well as that of others- so you are ready to respond in a God - honoring way. Angry words once spoken are not easily taken back.

Anger must be faced and the problems resolved so anger does not control you. Choose to forgive others and work out your problems so sin and lack of forgiveness can be avoided. Another response to anger is to choose not to be angry.

Some people like to use anger to control others. Choosing to forgive does not mean to continually allow others to use their temper on you and you forgive. God does not call you to maintain a close relationship with abusive people. He just asks you to forgive them and to receive healing from Him for your hurt.

WISDOM IN FORGIVENESS

Forgiveness does not automatically produce miraculous, instantaneous change. The forgiven person can still hold grudges or be under spiritual bondage. Listen for the still, quiet voice of the Holy Spirit for direction if you are to return to the relationship.

When my foster daughter prayed forgiveness for her sexually abusive father, I cautioned her that although she had forgiven him, it did not mean her relationship with her father was instantly or completely healed. She needed to wait for a strong confirmation of change.

She did not heed my warning and that evening she ran back into the arms of an unchanged, sexually-abusive father. We must be obedient and forgive. As with every prayer, we wait upon the leading of the Lord to know how, when or if the relationship is to be restored.

Sometimes we do not realize the need for forgiveness until an unpleasant memory roars unexpectedly to the surface. The memory could even be a nonverbal action such as withdrawal of affection or support at a particular time of great need. The person who acted in this matter can be totally unaware of the harm they have caused.

It is not necessary to point out every hurtful memory to others every time you forgive. Those who must constantly remind others they are forgiving them are just stroking their own pride and are not really forgiving.

Just forgive every time the memory is brought to mind, continue to forgive and to bless and to pray for healing until the pain is gone and and when you recall the memory there is no pain. You can remember but the pain has been removed from the memory.

Forgiveness is a life - time Kingdom attitude. Forgiveness is a Kingdom attitude of humbling ourselves. We continually choose such an attitude if we are to walk as Kingdom people.

THREE IMPORTANT ELEMENTS OF FORGIVENESS

(1) Hurt is not always one-sided even though from your perspective it may appear that way. Two people can see the hurt from different perspectives; It is easy to focus on self and misread others' intentions.

(2) Be aware your heart may hide hurt and the need for forgiveness. Ask God to reveal hidden areas in your heart of any hurt or unforgiveness.

(3) We always need to accept full responsibility for all of our actions. We are not to blame others or excuse ourselves for sinning due to past hurt.

If we have been offended, our wounds are fertile ground for keeping and growing hurt. When we hold on to our hurt it holds us back from freedom. Life becomes a rehash of the past and loses the promise of the future. Forgiving sets us free!

WAYS TO FORGIVE

When others have offended you, do not talk behind their back. Go to them and kindly let them know how you feel. This may be received several ways: they can respond by asking forgiveness, they may respond by not asking forgiveness, they may attempt to justify their actions or they may refuse to hear of their of their offenses.

THE MANIPULATOR

A manipulator is certain there is only one point of view - theirs! They cannot admit fault nor do they accept responsibility for their actions. They are blind to their own faults. Sometimes their actions appear gracious but they are only self - serving. Their actions contradict their words. If you should become suspicious, they often loudly claim offense, covering their actions with good-sounding excuses to make you appear the villain.

Do not be caught in this deception. These manipulators are using you! They play on emotions and, if their needs are not met, they move on to prey on other unsuspecting victims.

When we love with Kingdom covenant love, it is a strong love. We love unconditionally, but we do not allow our love, feelings or choices to be manipulated.

RECONCILIATION

Reconciliation can be the answer to some relationship problems. God offers His people the ministry of reconciliation (2 Corinthians 5:17-20). Reconciliation can happen with or without the actual confronting of hurts.

Sometimes the parties involved need to discuss the actual event and ask for forgiveness, but there are times when such a discussion would make resolving problems more complicated. Perhaps the two parties are coming from different perspectives. In this situation it is not who is right. You can agree to love and not allow your differences or misunderstandings to separate you. You can choose to allow love to be the basis for your relationship.

Sometimes people want to justify their position, making it harder for actual reconciliation to take place. Therefore, there are times when saying nothing but, "Let's be reconciled," is best. Sometimes, perhaps because of pride, immaturity or spiritual bondage, a person is unable to admit fault even though they know they are wrong. We can still stand for reconciliation and stand for love in that relationship. Which ever way God directs you to reconcile is the way you reconcile.

Once God told me to reconcile because the other person was not able to say they were sorry. This person wept publicly after being approached and simply asked, "can we reconcile?" Two months later he became Spirit - filled. As we forgive, we release people to God.

It is important to wait upon God's timing in these situations. I waited six months, but I did not move back into the relationship until prompted to do so by the Holy Spirit. The Spirit is faithful to prompt us to move when the time is right. We obey, and everything falls into place. There was a struggle as I waited though. I looked and searched diligently for what God would have me do. The waiting was not easy. But in this instance, the waiting brought great blessing.

Faithfully look for your answer, and you will recognize your answer when it comes. God is always faithful to answer our prayers and questions and His timing is perfect.

WHEN YOU HAVE DONE ALL - STAND

Many years ago, I heard a young lady share a vision that emphasized the importance of standing in the right place at the right time. In the vision, this person observed a large crowd of people streaming up the pathway to the top of a mountain. She blended into, and become a part of the crowd. As the crowd reached the top, they saw an open pathway that led to the edge of a sheer cliff. On the edge of the cliff stood Christians forming a human barrier to prevent those in the throng from simply falling over the ledge.

This lady saw a place on the edge of the cliff designated for her. She made her way through the throng to join other Christians on the edge of the mountain cliff as part of the human barrier. But there were places on the edge of the cliff where no one stood. In those places people poured through the gaps, careening over the sheer bluff.

This vision aptly describes how, as part of the body of Christ, we each have a definite place to stand. In standing, we form a human barrier to prevent those who are not Christians, (and those who are Christians but have lost their way) from falling off their cliff.

The Word states that when you have done all else, stand (Ephesians 6:11-17). To stand means to stay where you are and pray for another. It means to stand, immovable in prayer, until you have the answer for that person or it can be just simply not moving until the Spirit directs you to move. For example: moving out of a ministry or leaving a church body or a friendship. It can mean that just your physical presence is part of your prayer.

There are times to stand silently in prayer, never allowing another to know you are praying. You can pray forgiveness because they are not praying for themselves or do not see the need to pray. Forgive hurt inflicted on you or on others. Pray until you and others are healed. Bless them and demand that any evil spirits involved be bound. Stand praying, loving unconditionally and interceding for them before God. You are standing and preventing them from falling over the edge of that cliff. You guard and pray carefully for this person. They may be in such a battle or emotional turmoil, approaching them openly to discuss any issues would only stir up animosity. Love unconditionally and leave the rest to Jesus. This is a quiet, yet active, stand in prayer.

There are times you stand in the midst of a problem in order to view the problem clearly so you can determine when and how to pray. If you leave the situation too quickly you will not recognize where prayer is needed. God often calls His people to stand in difficult places until further notice. God teaches us valuable lessons as we follow His purpose and voice, waiting for the Spirit to confirm the time to move on (Proverbs 16:3).

Sometimes, after you have stood in prayer or in a position for a season, God urges you to move physically away from the people you have been near to, or for whom you have prayed. Perhaps God called you to intercede, but He lets you know when a job is finished.

Once I stood in prayer for a ministry, even becoming part of that ministry. I had to stand there to see the need for prayer. After about three months, to my complete surprise, I knew the time was over. Knowing this, I did not move, but continued to physically stand in prayer two more months waiting for confirmation. One evening, some friends came to visit. As they left, the husband turned to me and, completely out of context, stated vehemently, "It is time for you to return to where you were!" It was as if someone physically kicked a stool out from under my feet. I knew my "stand" was gone and I was free to leave. I let the church I was attending, knowing God was moving me on. I had only been there briefly to help pray.

If you attend and support a ministry, you need to stand with that ministry in positive prayer. Every ministry will have its problems, just because people are people. Whatever ministry you are a part of, you share your anointing - the gifting the Holy Spirit has given you - with them. You are to be there and share until the Holy Spirit moves you on. But do not continue to lend your anointing once the Spirit has directed you to move on. Sometimes you move where God needs you, sometimes the Spirit moves you out of a ministry for reasons you do not fully understand until later.

In I Samuel 15:10-26, King Saul lied to the prophet Samuel and disobeyed the Lord. Saul passed the blame onto others for his disobedience. The prophet Samuel, who previously had supported Saul, laid bare Saul's disobedience. At that point the prophet could no longer stand with Saul nor support Saul with his prophetic gifts.

God calls this blame passing, "witchcraft." You can hear this spirit of witchcraft in people when you hear them constantly blaming others and never accepting responsibility for their part.

LOVING, FORGIVING AND BLESSING YOUR OWN FLESH
THE MARRIAGE COVENANT

In the beginning God created man (and woman) in His own image. God blessed them and said, "Be fruitful and increase in number, fill the earth and subdue it. Rule over the fish of the sea, and the birds of the air and over every living creature (Genesis 27-31)."

The sexual relationship between one man and one woman establishes the marriage covenant. This covenant is holy in the eyes of God and exclusive (Romans 1:24-32). The Song of Solomon is an example of this holy relationship. It proclaims pure love in its' spontaneity, beauty, power and exclusiveness. God intends that this kind of passionate love be a normal part of marital life.

The man is to leave his father and his mother and become one with his wife (Genesis 1:26-31). How the two become one is a mystery but the man is commanded to love his wife as he loves himself and the wife is to respect her husband (Ephesians 5:32-33).

When Adam ate of the fruit in the garden of Eden he opened the entryway for the curse. Jesus came and broken this curse so that the blessing God gave to the husband and the wife can be restored. In this relationship the woman is not underneath her husband. Being underneath the man is living under the curse (Genesis 3:16).

Being one, and walking side-by-side, married couples guard how they pray and talk about each other. Negative prayers or constant criticism only increases problems. Being one, if you pray (speak) blessing, you receive blessing. This does not mean to ignore reality. But pray knowing reality and choose to love, to forgive, to bless and to be healed. This is Kingdom love. The kind of love that changes lives.

The husband is to cover and protect his wife. Together they pray and speak blessing to each other, blessing for their children, relatives, work situations and common needs.

CHILDREN

A pattern of constant, negative thoughts or statements from parents to their children reaches into the future, and can act like curses. Negative thinking about your children can work like negative prayers. Children need to be released into the hands of their heavenly Father they are, after all, His children first. God will covenant with you for every one of your children.

We know that love always hopes, always perseveres. Love prays the answers - not the problems.

PRAYER OF BLESSING
In the Name of Jesus I choose to pray blessing on _____ (name of child or spouse).
I bless them in the following ways _____, _____, _____.
God please forgive their rebellion and I pray they will turn their hearts towards You. Amen

---

"My Spirit, who is on you, and My words that I have put in your mouth, will not depart from your mouth, or from the mouths of your children, or from the mouths of their descendants from this time on and forever," says the Lord (Isaiah 59:21).

FORGIVING OURSELVES

All have sinned and fallen short of the Glory of God (Romans 3:23). However, *there is no condemnation for those who are in Christ Jesus* (Romans 8:1).

Because God completely forgives us, who are we not to forgive ourselves? When we feel convicted of sin it is time to seek forgiveness in prayer through confessing sin, thereby reconciling ourselves to God. If we still feel the guilt, we may need to confess the sin to another (James 5:16). Sometimes guilt lifts with an open confession - a very powerful kind of confession. As long as sin hides within, the enemy is allowed to torment. Once it is out in the open, the enemy loses his power to use guilt against us.

When we feel conviction, we need to repent. Condemnation, however, is not from God. When we condemn ourselves or others condemn us, we feel a great weight of guilt. Our eyes are focused upon self and not on God. Condemnation becomes a point of self-centeredness, a destructive cycle. We have to forgive and let go, breaking the destructive cycle by accepting God's provision for forgiveness. If the enemy of your soul returns to torment you with condemnation, return to this prayer and date it.

PRAYER OF FORGIVENESS
Lord forgive me for _____ (sin[s] committed).
I repent of my actions and thank You for helping me destroy
the influences of this sin on my life. Amen.

SOUL TIES

Soul ties are emotional connections that bind you to another person. You may not even realize they exist, but if you pray for release, God will grant it.

These ties influence the mind, will and emotions. Whenever you enter into a personal relationship with another such as a parent, surrogate parent, relative, strong friend, cult leader or sexual partner, a strong, emotional tie develops.

This emotional tie can cause a person to ignore their true, personal feelings or decisions in order to please, appease or receive acceptance from another. If you are in such a relationship, this sin needs to be confessed. If there has been victimization or overly strong emotional ties, these can be cut if one of the people involved prays.

Cutting these ties allows people the freedom to make their own decisions without pressure and without their free will being violated. Soul ties need to be cut between parents and their parents, children and their parents, good friends, pastors and any others the Holy Spirit brings to mind.

If you have been married more than once, you have became one flesh with your previous spouse. If you entered into a sexual relationship outside your marriage, you became one flesh with that person.

Soul ties must be cut and eliminated from a previous marriage(s) and/or the out-of-wedlock sin, along with repenting through confession. These and all the above emotional bondages, left in place, will prevent the exercise of free will. The person will stay under the influence of another and never truly be free. The greatest gift God gives is freedom.

Recognize that the person you have cut ties from may continue to want to control you. They will not be happy with you when you are free from their control. This will challenge their comfort zone. You will have to stand firm (kindly) in your resolve to stay free.

> **BREAKING SOUL TIES**
> In the Name of Jesus, I sever all emotional ties that hold me captive. Specifically, I sever soul ties between myself and _____ (name of person[s]). I ask forgiveness for allowing this tie to compromise my relationship with You, Jesus. Thank You, Lord, for freeing me so I might follow only You and give complete allegiance of my heart to You. Amen!

JUDGMENTS

Do not judge, or you, too, will be judged. For in the same way you judge others you will be judged and with the measure you use, it will be measured to you (Matthew 7:12).

Negative words can bind others. When we judge others, we must repent of our careless words and pray all negative judgments stop and their power be broken. Remember, there is only one Lawgiver, one Judge (James 4:12). The words with which you judge others will come upon you (Matthew 7:1).

We have the key to both bind and loose others with our words, prayers or judgments. We want to bind what is not of God and loose into the lives of others what is of God (Matthew 16:19).

God gives us the keys of the Kingdom of Heaven and whatever we bind on earth will be bound in heaven; And whatever we loose on earth will be loosed in heaven (Matthew 16:19).

Not only can we judge others, but others can judge us. Christians and non-Christians alike can judge and bind us, casting doubt on our reputation. Their words have power and can cause confusion. A sense of heaviness and doubt, like a dark cloud, can cover and oppress us, causing us to feel guilty - but not understand why. If you recognize these symptoms, pray that the power of their judgments would stop. You will feel a great heaviness lift, and such prayer is often followed by tremendous blessings (that were previously withheld because of judgments against you).

We are also capable of placing judgments upon ourselves. "I am sick and tired! Why am I so stupid? I will never understand!"

Our ears hear these things, and the body responds to our self-judgments. We need to repent and ask forgiveness for self-imposed curses. Pray negative judgments cease. Stop using negative language!

Your family or peers may have judged you, because judgments can follow through a generation or be continued through verbal abuse. Parents, peers or teachers may have planted curses into your mind and spirit when you were a young child. These negative words can continue to produce negative results. "You're worthless, a failure, no good, stupid, fat, ugly." These or other words can result in your unwittingly accepting those judgments.

A teacher could have harmfully labeled you by repeatedly calling you a "slow learner!" You then file away this judgment in your memory, accepting it as truth until you pray and break this judgment.

You can judge others: labeling them, judging their motives, decisions or commitment. Sometimes it is not what is said, but the inflection or tone of voice used. Learn to speak truth without using a judgmental tone.

As well as loosing yourself from judgment you also need to forgive those who have judged you. Whether you have given or accepted judgment, you can pray:

> **BREAKING JUDGMENTS AND CURSES**
> In the Name of Jesus, I command any judgments coming to me from _____ (name of person[s]) to stop. These judgments are to be broken and no longer influence my life or the life of those in my family. I stand and freely forgive. Also, forgive me for all the judgments I have made against _____ (name of person[s] you have judged). I repent for judging them and now release them from all my judgments. God, I pray you will bless them. Amen!

You can also use this prayer to break judgments made against you by churches, cities, civic or governmental groups. Check back into your life where you first noticed major change in health or finances. Find the source where confusion or torment entered. You can also reverse this curse, using Jeremiah 31:3.

When you choose to use the supernatural love of Jesus, practice forgiveness, use wisdom in relationships, bless your marriage partner and your children, loose judgments and reconcile relationships, you beat the ground with zeal and defeat the wiles of the enemy. You truly are taking God's Kingdom by love and thereby releasing His Kingdom here on earth.

THE KING'S EDICT
Bless those who curse you and pray
for those who spitefully use you.

FAITH - KINGDOM PRINCIPLES

Without faith it is impossible to please God, because anyone who comes to Him must believe that He exists, and that He rewards those who earnestly seek Him (Hebrews 11:6).

God speaks and, by faith, we respond. We believe God is who He says He is, and will do what He says He will do. How do we activate faith? Faith is a choice - an action in word or deed. It is an action of obedience to God. This action then makes substance of things that did not exist before. Faith is the substance - maker of God's Kingdom.

FAITH AS A CHOICE

Faith is a choice, just as love is a choice. You can choose to believe God and act on that choice, believe in that choice and set your course by that choice. The choice to believe or act should not be determined by feelings or circumstances. The great patriarch of the Old Testament, Abraham, is an excellent life to examine. Abraham is considered the Father of Faith because he believed God.

Abraham believed God and it was credited to him as righteousness (Romans 4:3b). It was not through the law that Abraham and his offspring received the promise he would be heir of the world, but through the righteousness that comes by faith (Romans 4:13).

Because of Abraham's faith he received the promise that he would be heir of the world. When you choose faith you win ground for you and your children. What if you don't feel as if you believe?

Feelings are not necessarily important in the faith factor. Feelings can be fickle. Sometimes feelings can rise in great emotional fervor and then one is ready to believe. However if God were to speak a rhema word to you and your feelings were not stimulated, respond based on God - not on your feelings. If you choose to believe God, your feelings will align with your choices.

You can experience doubt and still have faith. Doubt is a feeling, and feelings come and go. They are neither right nor wrong. Only as you act on the wrong feelings are actions wrong. You express faith as you act upon God's Word. Even Abraham had anxious moments, but God did not count them against him (Romans 4:19 and footnote).

Circumstances can be deceptive. It can appear as if you are on the wrong road heading away from the prize of God's Kingdom. True, you might have chosen differently, but God is in control. Recognize it is God, not circumstances that determine your destiny. God uses circumstances to teach you, and these circumstances can include suffering. Everyone experiences difficult circumstances. Difficult circumstances are opportunities to believe God is in charge and opportunities to speak God's word back to Him in faith.

PRAYER OF FAITH

Lord I believe in what Your Word states: that in all things, whether good or bad, God will bring good to those who love Him and are called according to His purposes (Romans 8:28). Therefore I give thankgiving and praise ahead of time for the good You will bring to me. Amen.

You possess the Kingdom of Heaven through the physical action of making your feelings follow your choices and by knowing God is in charge of all of your circumstances. Faith is walking in belief that God is the all - powerful, almighty God of the universe and He is faithful to perform His Word. Fear is the antithesis of faith.

Take the story of Noah as an example of faith (Genesis 6:11-9:1). Noah had a rhema word from God, "Build an ark!" Noah responded by building an ark on dry land. Noah was not a boat builder. He became a boat builder in response to God's rhema word. He was obedient to perform the word God gave him. When Noah rode in the ark above the waters, he was a man who had built a boat. When his ark of faith landed, Noah literally owned the whole world. If we obey God and build our ark of faith, we will literally inherit the world when we land.

God works through His Kingdom principles of faith. When one chooses to apply the principles of faith, they are beating the ground for God's Kingdom to be established on earth as it is in heaven.

The following are some Kingdom principles to respond to with physical acts or actions. (You have an advocate with the Father, so when you make mistakes you can ask forgiveness and begin again.) The principles do not include the rhema Word of God, because each of us can receive different rhema words. The principles are, Seek first God's Kingdom, the Sabbath Rest, Power of our Words, Speaking to Circumstances, Stewardship, Giving, Reaping and Sowing, Discipleship, Submission, Unity and Honor. There are assuredly more principles; however, as you begin, take careful note. Principles are not to be valued above relationship! Principles are simply outward actions performed out of love. The relationship is always the priority! The reason you are privy to the relationship, Kingdom living and Kingdom success is only because of the blood sacrifice of Jesus. You are just an imperfect, saved person on your Kingdom journey learning Kingdom principles.

SEEK FIRST THE KINGDOM

Seek first His Kingdom and His righteousness, and all these things will be given to you as well (Matthew 6:33).

We are not to worry about what we will eat, drink or what clothes we will wear, for as you seek His Kingdom and His righteousness, all these things will follow. But first seek God's Kingdom! In seeking first God's Kingdom, you must set aside all other kingdoms.

THE SABBATH REST

There remains, then, a Sabbath - rest for the people of God. Anyone who enters God's rest, also rests from his own work, just as God did from His (Hebrews 4:9-10).

The people Moses led out of the bondage of Egypt were not able to enter God's rest, The Promised Land, because of their unbelief and the hardness of their hearts. They wandered in the desert forty years until all those who did not believe died (Deuteronomy 1:26-36).

When the last of this unbelieving generation died, Joshua delivered the new generation (those who believed God) into the Promised Land. Joshua was convinced of the power of God's promises to overcome the circumstances of giants and other difficulties confronting him. Joshua had the faith to believe when God told him to only be strong and courageous, and every place where his foot touched God would give to him (Joshua 1:1-9).

You, too, have been delivered out of bondage. Today, if you hear His voice, harden not your hearts (Hebrews 4:7). As with Joshua, only be strong and courageous and every place upon which you tread, God will give to you. Believe in God not your circumstances.

Believe that God is. Believe He rewards those who diligently seek Him. And, no matter what the circumstances, choose to believe Him. In choosing to believe God, you activate faith and enter into the promised rest: a rest without condemnation.

THE POWER OF OUR WORDS

A wise man's heart guides his mouth. Proverbs 16:23

In our tongue is the power of life and death. Be careful not to pattern your speech after the speech of the world (Proverbs 18:20,21; Numbers 14:26-29; Matthew 12:35-37). Being critical is not of God.

With our mouth we commit to bless people not curse them. If I am driving in my car and someone cuts in front of me and I swear at them, I am cursing them. We are made in God's image and we are not to curse that image (Genesis 1:26; James 3:9, Genesis 9:6 see footnote). Constant criticism is very destructive. It causes great injury.

If you speak behind someone's back your careless words bring judgments, and the person stands judged by your words. If you have something to say, say it with kindness and honesty to them. They then have the opportunity to respond. Walk very carefully. Not everything needs to be to spoken. Honesty is not an excuse to abuse verbally. Most often just release things through prayer.

Do everything without complaining or arguing, so that you may become blameless and pure, children of God, without fault, in a crooked and depraved generation, in which you shine like stars in the universe as you hold out the Word of life (Philippians 2:14).

Those using Kingdom words do not seek to build self - esteem or self - reliance for that is building up the kingdom of self. God's perspective is to speak His plan into the hearts of others until it is revealed. These are not empty words but creative faith words. Because God has called His people from the womb for a purpose and a destiny, we simply agree with God. We then invest ourselves in His perspective. When God has given a promise, instead of saying, "It will never happen," speak the promise back to God. God, hearing your belief, will respond.

Using the tongue's creative power does not mean just to be a positive speaker in order to manipulate others or God, but it means agreeing with God and confessing His perfect purpose.

SPEAKING TO A CIRCUMSTANCE

If circumstances feel overpowering, we have the authority to command them to come under our feet. Everything is under the feet of Jesus, and as co-heirs with Jesus, we have that same authority (Ephesians 1:20-23, Romans 8:17).

SPEAKING TO CIRCUMSTANCES
In the Name of Jesus I command these circumstances
_____ to move underneath my feet! Amen.

Focus on Jesus. Insist circumstances move. The circumstances may not change, but you now stand with a different perspective. Peter walked above his circumstances when he walked on water. As long as Peter kept his eyes on Jesus, he never sank. Only as he looked away was he overwhelmed (Matthew 14:25-31).

Jesus reveals His authority over these circumstances: temptation (Matthew 4:1-11), nature (Matthew 21:18-19), water, wind (Matthew 8:23-27), animals (Mark 11:1-3) and fish (Luke 5:1-11), food (Matthew 14:13-21; 15:32), this world and trouble (John 16:33), demons, disease (Matthew 4:24), death (John 11:38-44) and the impossible (Mark 10:27).

STEWARDSHIP

More is given to those who are good stewards because they know it belongs to God's Kingdom. It is a trust to be used for Kingdom purposes. Therefore, If you see a brother without a coat, give him one of yours (Matthew 5:40-48). We are called to be disciples. A disciple is a professed follower of Christ and a good steward over all God gives.

GIVING TO GOD

Giving to the Lord reveals where our allegience lies: in ourselves, in the world or in God. Giving to God is not law, rather, it is a Kingdom principle. (Mark 12:38-40 speaks harshly concerning those who teach Christianity based on Old Testament Law.) Giving is faithfully placing our fiancial-well being in God's Kingdom where His Monetary System rules.

Whoever sows sparingly will also reap sparingly and whoever sows generously will also reap generously. Each man should give what he has decided in his heart to give, not reluctantly or under compulsion for God loves a cheerful giver. And God is able to make all grace abound to you so that in all things at all times, having all that you need, you will abound in every good work (2 Corinthians 9:6-15).

REAPING AND SOWING

For every Kingdom action there is a reaction. Whatever you are planting into your life or the lives of others - whether it is faith, the Word of God, forgiveness, charity or finances - you will receive back if you sow as God directs. Sow generously as the Holy Spirit prompts, and do not give up, and you will reap generously (Galatians 6:7-10).

The opposite is also true: The negative things you plant will yield an infected crop. If you have been sowing negativity, repent and turn. For a while you may still reap from negative seeding. If, for example, you have been a thief but have decided to stop stealing, you may have to pay through the criminal courts.

DISCIPLESHIP

Salvation is a free gift, but if you want to be a disciple, you pay a price. The price is letting go of your own will to follow in God's way. This is not always an easy choice but it is a very beneficial choice.

The free grace Jesus offers cost Him everything. If we take that sacrifice lightly and go about our own business, we are not true disciples (Luke 14:25-28).

HONOR, SUBMISSION AND UNITY

Give honor to those whom honor is due. The first to honor is your parents. This is the only commandment with a promise: Honor your father and your mother so that you may live long in the land the Lord is giving you. To honor is to respect, esteem and to make your parents proud by the way you live your life (Exodus 20:12). In honoring your parents, you honor God.

Submit to the Lord, your God, and follow Him with all your heart. If you are married, your spouse becomes sanctified by your choice.

(1 Corinthians 7:14). Jesus gave His life so that what Adam lost in the Garden of Eden would be restored - man and woman walking together as one. Submit one to another, live in unity, for where there is unity, God bestows His blessing (Psalm 133:1-3, Romans 15:5-6).

ACCOUNTABILITY

Wives are to be accountable and faithful to their husbands. Husbands are to be accountable and faithful to God and to their wives. Children are to be accountable to their parents. Pastors are to be accountable to God for the people God gives into their care (Proverbs 31:10-33, 20:6; Ephesians 5:22-25, 6:1-3, 4:11-13).

If you are a disciple, know that disciples are faithful at their place of work and they cheerfully pay bills and taxes on time (Matthew 22:21). These things are a matter of practice. God appreciates it when we practice. God is not looking for perfection, but He looks to find those who have willing hearts to learn. Hearts that prove trustworthy.

Disciples are people of the Word. They are to be accountable and faithful to perform their words and promises in a timely fashion and not to speak careless, empty words. The world is watching to see if Christians speak empty words or if they are really doers of their words.

FAITH AS AN ATTITUDE

We know that in all things God works for the good of those who love the Him, who have been called according to His purpose (Romans 8:28).

Faith is an attitude of gratitude, thanksgiving and praise toward God. The Word of God repeatedly admonishes and encourages us to praise God in all things. We can praise God through music, verbal words of praise, thanksgiving and worship. Faith is an attitude we can choose to develop. Faith is an attitude that pleases God.

MUSIC

Music can bypass the mind and move uncensored into the soul. Music touches your emotions as little else can and is, therefore, a powerful force in and out of the Kingdom.

According to Bernice Regan Johnson, music can have a positive influence on the air through which it travels and upon those the air touches. In her interview program aired on Public Broadcasting System, "The Songs are Free," Mrs. Johnson relates how, during the 60's, Gospel music was a major factor in easing racial tensions. Police, tenement owners and shop owners witnessed freedom rallies attended by blacks, where the air felt thick and oppressive. If someone started an old Gospel hymn, however, voices would quickly be raised in unison and praise. The song would fill the air, nullifying the intense anger.

Praise music can be used as a tool. You claim God's Kingdom by praising the name of Jesus. Praise pulls down the strongholds of the enemy and takes space.

PRAISE

We praise because of who God is and who God is to us, not to manipulate. Praising to receive only what you want is manipulation, and God will not be tricked. If you use words of praise simply as words of conversation, they become ineffective as either praise or conversation.

Because a grateful heart moves the hand of God and brings good out of all bad situations, this Kingdom principle activates the miraculous. You have relationship with God, and although evil surrounds you, it will be used for your good. We do not operate on the same level as the world, but upon Kingdom principles. God is God and He can bring about good, whether you praise Him or not. He brings about good and therefore, you can praise Him.

Praise breaks the hold of the enemy. The enemy cannot stand praise! He will vacate the space. Therefore we are to praise, not considering circumstances, but give a sacrifice of praise through our difficult times, lifting up the name of Jesus.

Sometimes, especially when we are complaining and whining, we need an attitude adjustment. Because praise is a choice - an attitude of gratitude - when you choose to praise, your attitude changes.

These are some of the different kinds of praise: sacrificial praise, praising God because He is good, praising just because God is who He says He is and is our all in all, praising out of gratitude and praising to enter into God's presence.

WORSHIP

Worship occurs as you enter into a higher place of praise. Worship leads us into a holy place, the very throne room of God. You enter into an intimate place, a place where you touch His very presence.

Music, praise and worship are power - packed gifts for bringing our petitions and needs before God, power - packed ways to tear down the strongholds of the prince of the air (Satan). As the air around us is filled with praise, it changes the air and the people in that air.

The enemy cannot tolerate us praising God and will flee from where true praise and worship are being offered. I have witnessed miracles as I praised God in difficult circumstances, sometimes even through tears. The biggest miracle of all is the change He accomplishes in my heart as I act in obedience to His Word.

Suffering is real, and there will be times and seasons to praise through suffering. There is also a need to know and practice spiritual warfare and, to use wisdom (so you are not the cause of self-inflicted suffering due to lack of wisdom).

THE SERVANT

You know that the rulers of the Gentiles lord it over them, and their high officials exercise authority over them. Not so with you! Instead, whoever wants to become great among you must be your servant, and whoever wants to be first must be your slave. Just as the Son of Man did not come to be served, but to serve, and to give His life as a ransom for many (Matthew 20:25-28).

You should not only have an attitude of gratitude, but your attitude should also be that of an obedient servant. You are called to serve. You are to worship the Lord, your God, and Him alone (Matthew 4:10), serving Him with your whole heart. Jesus submitted His own will, even unto death, to serve at the Father's command. Jesus was the perfect example of a servant King. In serving God, you wait upon Him, prepare your hearts for Him and allow Him the opportunity to speak and direct your life. Serve God and serve each other in love (Galatians 5:13). When you serve in love you truly have a servant's heart.

However, you are to serve only when and where God calls. If you serve when you are not called, you serve only self. This type of service does not please God. Therefore we are not to take upon ourselves things to do simply because someone else says that we are supposed to do them, or because of our area of gifting. In all areas we are to wait upon the Lord and lend our ear to the direction He has for our lives. We become a servant of the Lord, not a servant to man or to self. As servants of the Lord, we walk as Kingdom people.

FAITH AS SUBSTANCE

Faith comes by hearing and hearing by the Word of God. Faith is the evidence of things not yet seen. When one has faith or belief that God will do what He has promised, a deposit (literally) is made into their account in the Kingdom of Heaven. Now, those of faith and their offspring, can draw on this account (Romans 4:3, 4:13).

Abraham exhibited faith and God counted it to him as righteousness. What is true for Abraham is true for us also (Romans 4:23-24, Romans 4:16 see footnotes). God will credit faith as righteousness to us and to our children as we believe in Him and act accordingly.

HOPE - THE PROMISE OF THE KINGDOM

Hope is a place, a relationship and a future. If you place your hope in the things of this world, or yourself, instead of Christ, you can lose hope very quickly. To lose hope is to live in a place of devastation, with nothing to live for. Hope is keeping your eyes on Jesus, the one who is your hope.

You have hope that you will become all God has called you to be. You can have hope in God, as God honors those who serve Him, and God rewards those who earnestly seek Him (Hebrews 11:6).

You hope for yourself as you place your hope in Christ and find in Him an anchor of safety, for it is safe to hope in Jesus. In Him you can find a relationship and a destiny. God will never forget us, as He has carved our names on the palm of His hands (Isaiah 49:15-16). Within this relationship there is stability and security.

Every son whom God accepts is disciplined (kept in line) for their own safety (Hebrews 12:5-11). God is in this for the long term and He builds character in us through suffering and perseverance. In and through everything God continually gives His people hope.

God builds character and hope into His citizens. Suffering produces perseverance, perseverance produces character and character produces hope (Romans 5:3-5).

INTERCESSION

You can hope for family, friends, strangers or for your city, country and leaders, interceding for them in prayer. When others have no hope, you commit to hope for them as you stand faithfully before God in prayer for their future. Hope is the bright promise of the Kingdom.

Intercession is repenting for the sins of others, asking forgiveness for their sins and standing in the place of prayer for them. Yes, they must also personally repent, but you prepare the way by asking God to forgive. Jesus modeled this action of forgiveness from the Cross when He said, "Father, forgive them for they know not what they do."

You can also hope for them through the Isaiah 58 Fast or physical fasting. When you practice hope for them you beat the ground for them because they did not have the strength for themselves. So you beat the ground with great zeal until the snakes leave and the one you have held out hope for can finally see the Kingdom of God.

This is not typical prayer; it involves a struggle. Pray, praise and quote the Word. Be led by the Spirit. Be sure your heart is clean before God. Be attentive to listen to the Holy Spirit.

Every prayer within this text can be used as intercessory prayer for spouses, children and parents. The index for all prayers is found in the front of *The Kingdom*.

FASTING

The kind of fast the Lord requires of us is to first have charity, love and consideration for others. Fasting without charity is only an outward action, producing nothing of lasting value. There are several different ways to fast. Consider the Isaiah 58 Fast as one that offers great blessing and a fast that God, Himself, recommends.

THE ISAIAH 58 FAST

Is not this the kind of fasting I have chosen: to loose the chains of injustice, untie the cords of the yoke, to set the oppressed free and break every yoke?

Is it not to share your food with the hungry? Provide the poor wanderer with shelter? When you see the naked, to clothe him? And do not turn away from your own flesh and blood.

Then your light will break forth like the dawn, your healing will quickly appear, your righteousness will go before you and the Glory of the Lord will be your rear guard.

Then when you call, the Lord will answer; you will cry for help, and the Lord will say: "Here I am (Isaiah 58:6-9)!"

Therein lies a true fast, one that is born out of love and sacrifice. There are also physical fasts. They can include certain parts of a day or week, whole days, certain foods.

A fast can be in response to a call from the Holy Spirit, for the nation, others or for yourself. Fasting is a matter of continually choosing to be obedient. As with anything be aware of your own limitations. A diabetic individual, for example, should not skip meals.

When one fasts, it is not to be done publicly, but quietly and unto the Lord (Matthew 6:16-18). Jesus puts food into perspective in John 4.

"My food is to do the will of Him who sent me and to finish His work" (John 4:34).

HOPE FOR OUR NATION

You can hope for your nation. You hope by praying and fasting and turning from your sin, by praying and repenting personally for the forgiveness of the sin of your city, your nation. God promises to hear these prayers and heal your land. Healing of the land is not dependent upon those in the world. Healing of the land is dependent upon followers of Jesus like you and me and our prayers before God. We are the ones responsible for the state of the nation, because we have not stood in prayer, in faith and repentance. God calls it our responsibility.

Healing of the land is conditional (often God gives conditional promises in Scripture). We have a specific part to perform before God will obligate Himself to fulfill the promise given.

If My People *will humble themselves and pray, seek My face and turn from their wicked ways, then will I hear from heaven, forgive their sin and heal their land (2 Chronicles 7:14).*

There are five conditions for healing of our nation: we first must be His people, humble ourselves, pray, continue to seek His face and turn from our our wicked ways. Then God obligates Himself torespond to our prayers.

We have a part and God has a part. We took to choosing to do our part first. God gives His Word that He will fulfill His part once His conditions are met.

SIGNS AND WONDERS, THE FAVOR OF GOD, AND PROPHECY

Signs and wonders accompany the believer; therefore, as a believer, you can expect them to follow you (Mark 16:17). You can pray for favor from God and man. Jesus found favor with both so we can find favor with both (Luke 2:52; Exodus 12:36).

You can give others hope and build them up in their most holy faith by agreeing with them, prophesying over them, exhorting them and supporting them to believe in the destiny God has for their lives and thereby supporting them in their vision.

THE ESSENCE OF HOPE

You find hope in God and hope in God's Word. God places hope in your heart before you even really know Him. Hope is that energizing force that keeps you moving ever forward and closer to God who is the source of all hope. God gives hope in His Word. You can bring hope into actual substance by speaking God's Word in all circumstances. You must choose to speak God's Word rather than your own words of defeat. It is how you choose life and blessing.

Though speech, you subject your most unruly member (your tongue) into agreement with Creator God and gain control over the physical realm. As you persist in this action, the physical circumstances around you have to conform to God's Word. Literally, you are changing the physical world into God's Kingdom through the words of your mouth. It is a choice you can make. (As discussed previously, praising in all circumstances is also a powerful means to take physical ground.) Hope, just as love and faith, is a choice.

May the God of hope fill you with all joy and peace as you trust in Him, so that you may overflow with hope by the power of the Holy Spirit (Romans 15:13).

REVIEW AND PROJECT

Throughout Chapter Five, choices, principles and actions are placed before you to reveal God's Kingdom. Know that the examples given are not the only ways the Spirit works.

As you apply these teachings, they will open your eyes to the freedom of Kingdom living and, the Spirit will open your eyes to any additional principles He wants you to learn. It is your faith journey.

God gives us the gift of free will and then He gives us choices. God's Kingdom is a Kingdom where love is a choice, faith is a choice, hope is a choice and obedience is a choice. You choose and go forward with persistence and determination willing to obey God.

The three unchangeable standards in the Kingdom are: Love, faith and hope. In choosing to love you have discovered the only law and the heartbeat of God'sKingdom. In choosing faith you make substance using Kingdom principles calling into being those things that are not. In choosing hope you plug into the energizing force - the promise of the Kingdom. In choosing to listen and obey God's rhema word for you you choose to inherit these promises. God knows that as you put into practice these choices, you will truly realize freedom - a freedom and a joy you never before knew existed.

God's Kingdom is not a Kingdom built on natural law, neither is it earned by natural law. (Important: Read Galatians 3.) His is a spiritual Kingdom built on spiritual principles. You make Kingdom choices in the supernatural and then what you have acquired in the supernatural becomes substance in the natural - substance for you and for your family.

You participate in God's Kingdom as you exercise your free will and call forth His Kingdom and continue to call forth His Kingdom until your experience of the Kingdom becomes true reality.

In not making any choices or knowing about the choices but not really seizing them for yourself, you stay under the sentence of death and the curse. Why would you want to stay there when faith sets you free? You can choose life or death, blessing or cursing. It is entirely up to you. Beginning this very day, let it be said of you, that you have chosen wisely.

Know that in all His grace is sufficient for you. For it is by grace that we are saved, not by our works. No man can boast about earning anything from God. Heaven/Salvation/Eternity are His gifts to us. Jesus already paid the price on the cross. Therefore, we live by grace, not legalistically following the law. The relationship is always to be our upmost priority. Godly principles are merely guidelines. They let us know how free we truly are and what a loving relationship we have with God. It is a relationship where He guides, teaches and leads us personally and we freely love obey and follow Him in return.

I ask that you love one another and this is love: that we walk in obedience to His commands. And you have heard from the beginning His command is that you walk in love (2 John 1:4-7).

Chapter Five reveals the standards of the Kingdom: love, faith and hope. Chapter Six is a study of God's healing for the body, soul and spirit of man.

6
The Kingdom Health Plan

Man is a triune creature: body, soul and spirit. The body is the physical, outward appearance; the soul includes the mind, will and emotions; and the spirit is where the Spirit of God resides. God's Kingdom Health Plan addresses healing for body, soul and spirit.

JOY AND WISDOM AS MEDICINE

A cheerful heart is good medicine, but a crushed spirit dries up the bones (Proverbs 17:22).

God has prescribed a large dose of His medicine for His children. This medicine is joy. Those who enter into that joy, even if they are unsure how this medicine works, will receive the benefits.

Joy is medicine for the body, just as laughter and songs of joy are part of deliverance (Psalm 126:1-6). God uses laughter as He routs the enemy (Psalm 2:4). Joy is an anointing (Psalm 45:7). We are filled with joy at the presence of God (Psalm 16:11). The presence of the Lord is the greatest blessing and the wellspring of all other blessings. If we are dwelling in the presence of the Lord we dwell in joy (Psalm 21:6).

Trust in the Lord with all your heart, lean not unto your own understanding. In all your ways acknowledge Him, and He will make your paths straight. Do not be wise in your own eyes; fear the Lord and shun evil. This will bring health to your body and nourishment to your bones (Proverbs 3:5-8).

HEALING FOR THE PHYSICAL BODY

Through the disobedience of the first man, Adam, a door was flung open and in marched disease and death.

The second Adam, Jesus, came to restore what the first Adam lost. Through an act of obedience, Jesus laid down His life as a blood sacrifice to pay for the restoration of God's Kingdom. Jesus paid for sin and now death and disease have their orders to retreat. Sin is the disease, the curse. In God's Kingdom you can exchange the curse for the blessing of life.

When Jesus Christ is your Lord and Savior, you enter into eternal life. When you accept Him as Healer you enter into health. Jesus has come and healing is His song. You obtain this song by learning to be a singer yourself. Persist until you become one with the song and one with the singer. The song of God's Kingdom is healing, the song is one of the greatest gifts of love, for it is a song of His love - God loving us while we are yet imperfect. As you receive healing, apply a generous amount of wisdom. If you are taking a prescription or are under a doctors' care, return to the doctor and have him confirm your healing.

Know it is the will of the King for those in His Kingdom to be healed. Jesus offers Kingdom healing. God provides a prayer for healing through the anointing of oil for the forgiveness of sins.

If anyone is sick he should call the elders of the church to pray over him and anoint him with oil in the name of Jesus. And the prayer offered in faith will make the sick person well. If he has (they have) sinned, he will (they will) be forgiven. Therefore, confess your sins to one another and pray for one another (James 5:13-15).

ANOINTING WITH OIL
In the Name of Jesus I anoint you with oil for healing from _____.

Jesus, provides healing through suffering and humiliation He endured on the Cross. On the Cross He took the penalty of sin that belongs to us (mankind), placed it upon Himself and paid our debt.

Surely He took up our infirmities and carried our sorrows, yet we considered Him stricken by God, smitten by Him and afflicted. But He was pierced for our trangressions, He was crushed for our iniquities the punishment that brought us peace is upon Him and by His wounds (upon the Cross), we are healed..........For the Lord has laid on Him the iniquity (that which we deserve) of us all (Isaiah 53:4 - 5).

> **PRAYER OF EXCHANGE**
> I thank you Lord Jesus, that You have paid my sin debt in full through Your willingness to suffer and die in my place. I receive the gift You have given and declare that by Your wounds I am healed. Amen!

God also heals through intercession or you may seek out some people given a gift of healing (gift of the Holy Spirit). God also heals through fasting (2 Chronicles 2:14), speaking the Words of God in all circumstances, a rhema Word of God, a Word of Knowledge (gift of the Holy Spirit), through faith (Luke 8:42-48), through faith of friends (Luke 5:18-26), to reveal His glory (John 11:4), through the natural remedies of doctors, exercise, vitamins, proper eating habits and rest.

If you have not received immediate healing, is that a reason not to trust God? Know that some healing is progressive, some healing may require you to stand in faith, some healing may be dependent upon healing of the soul and healing in the areas of the Spirit. Healing is not a magic formula, but rather is living in relationship with, Jesus, the Healer.

HEALING FOR THE SOUL

Healing for the soul is emotional healing - a process whereby Jesus touches and heals memories hidden in the depths of the human soul. The soul is the mind, will and emotions (heart). This kind of healing includes: forgivemess, cutting soul ties and judgments, eliminating bitter roots and rolling away stones of offense. God can also speak to you concerning needs through prophetic words, dreams and visions. The following pages suggest some specific area to consider healing for the soul (sometimes called Inner Healing). God's Word informs us that we are to be strengthened in our inner man.

He wants you to be strengthened in your inner man, so that Christ may dwell in your hearts through faith and you will be rooted and established in love and may have the power to grasp how wide and long and big and deep is the love of Christ (for you), and to know His love that surpassess knowledge that you may be filled to the measure of all the fullness of God (Ephesians 3:14-19).

THE HEART

The heart is deceitful, often hiding its true nature and feelings. Ask the Holy Spirit to reveal what is hidden in your heart so you can pray, confess your sin and receive healing. Ask God to give you a new heart (Ezekiel 36:24-26). Write the teachings of the Lord on the tablet of your heart (Proverbs 7:1-3).

ABANDONMENT

When a child is abandoned, they will suffer a spiritual hole in their heart - an area that becomes open for deception. It is a howling emptiness, for torment has been allowed access to the heart. Pray for the abandoned heart to be restored and healed. Because this person can consistently make poor choices in relationships, pray that discernment will be restored to the heart and that it will be protected. Pray forgiveness. Face the torment and in the name of Jesus, command it to leave. Psalm 147:3 teaches that God heals the brokenhearted and binds up their wounds and fills their emptiness with Himself. He becomes light where there was darkness and His light overcomes our darkness.

THE BROKEN HEART

A heart that has been hurt repeatedly will find it difficult to feel and accept love no matter how much love is given. A person in this situation needs to have prayer for their heart to heal.

God is close to those with a broken heart and will heal them (Psalm 34:18, 147:3). A broken heart comes from physical or verbal abuse, divorce, unfilled promises or broken relationships.

WALLS

Because of hurt, people can begin to build interior walls of safety for protection from further hurt. They may reach out and love, but they are prevented from really believing they are loved. These inside protective barriers prevent love from entering. These walls prevent one from growing up. Emotional development stops at the point where walls were established. The real person is trapped behind those walls. On the outside where everyone can view is a mask to hide the hurt. Inside is like a dark cave.

This hiding place was a place of safety as one lives through hurt - a way of coping with difficult circumstances and emotions when they knew of no other. But now is the time to be set free. But how?

First, pray for freedom by recognizing and/or admitting the walls, forgive those who contributed to the building of your walls and ask for healing. Visualize Jesus coming to help you remove your walls. See Jesus take your hand and lead you out of the dark place into His light. You will sense that the person you really wanted to be (who was trapped inside), is now free to be completely expressed. Your emotions can be pretty unpredictable once freed. You will have to learn anew how to manage them.

You will also become vulnerable to people and hurt. If you choose not to be vulnerable, you will not experience those deep emotions of being loved. You will be hurt again and again, but now you can deal with that hurt. It's a choice to come out from behind these walls. Once you know this process, you may see yourself building those walls back. Freedom is on the outside, and it is safe there with Jesus. Ask Jesus to reveal your walls, and then actively participate in keeping them down.

REJECTION FROM BIRTH

When a mother does not want her child and/or considers having an abortion, the child experiences rejection (Psalm 27:10). This root of rejection and bitterness forms in the heart of the child. There can even be a sense of death or wanting to die. That spirit of rejection, visible in anger and bitterness when the child is older, needs prayer and the command to depart. The root of bitterness needs to be confessed and then commanded to loose its grip and leave. Pray against a spirit of murder if abortion was considered. Truth needs to be placed into the spirit of the child or adult, so they know they are wanted and have been called forth from the womb by God (1 Peter 2:9-11).

BITTERNESS/BITTER ROOTS

Bitterness takes root when a person is hurt by broken promises or broken relationships. Pray, commanding roots of bitterness to shrivel up and die (Ephesians 4:31). Choose to be rooted and established in love (Ephesians 3:17). When you pray commanding bitterness to leave, you may experience a spitting up or bitter taste.

A BROKEN SPIRIT

Divorce* in a family can produce a broken spirit in a child. Their emotional growth stops. Recognize the broken area, stand, forgive and pray for the broken spirit to be healed. Know that it can be difficult as an adult for them to be faithful in a marriage, as divorce is always that easy option.

Divorce robs the child and they are thrown into a barren place where there are constant tormenting spirits. This barrenness is not easily recognized because it becomes so familiar. In this place, a tormenting spirit constantly drives them.

In this barren land lives a Dragon (Spirit of Jealousy). It is this spirit who constantly tears up their lives and destroys all the good they have planted. This is an area for deliverance, as well as Inner Healing. See *The Power - Christian Primary III* under The Spirit of Jealousy to break this hold. *The Rumors of Nard* is recommended reading for further information on this Spirit of Jealousy.

SHAME

The soul experiences shame for various reasons, most especially because of sexual abuse. It can also be caused from loss of job, position, others sinning in your family or personal sin. In these situations, pray for the soul to be healed, for forgiveness, for the removal of anger, for the healing of pain and for the shame to be removed from you and your family (Romans 9:33).

In Isaiah 61:7 there is found a precious promise for those who have experienced shame in their lives. They will inherit from the Lord a double portion.

Instead of their shame, my people will receive a double portion, instead of disgrace, they will rejoice in their inheritance and so they will inherit a double portion in their land and everlasting joy will be theirs (Isaiah 61:7).

---

*This does not mean a parent should stay in a relationship where there is physical abuse, sexual abuse (to children) or drug use, to avoid divorce. God can restore and give a new beginning for He is the God of New Beginnings. He is also the God of all knowledge and He delights in caring for His people, so ask for wisdom in how to proceed and God will be most faithful to direct.

THE BREACH

The seeds of disrespect can be sown into family members. Seeds of distrust may be planted into children because a wife disrespects her husband. As a result, the children do not honor or respect their parents. This breakdown of respect can follow generational lines, preventing children from having healthy, intimate, parental relationships.

This sin of disrespect and dishonor needs to be repented of and replaced with respect. Pray over the seeds of disrespect so they will no longer produce a negative harvest. Scripture teaches that whatever is sown will be reaped. It is God's desire for us to reap Kingdom benefits and receive all the blessings God's Kingdom offers. We participate with God when we sow respect and honor. It is a choice we can make. A choice we make not considering the condition of the person receiving respect. At the same time we walk with wisdom in the relationship and do not allow ourselves to be caught in an abusive situation.

GUILT

Guilt can be heavy emotional baggage, resulting from sin, inappropriate feelings of responsibility for a wrong (such as a divorce, a teenager's rebellion, loss of a job) or because others perceive us as guilty. For actual wrongs committed, sincerely ask for (and receive) God's forgiveness. Receiving God's forgiveness allows us to stop judging ourselves and let go of the guilt (1 John 1:7-9).

If others perceive you as guilty, and you are not, treat it as a judgment. Then, command their judgments of you to be broken and to leave.

THE SLUMBERING SPIRIT

At times a person can know God and have received salvation, but perhaps, due to devastation, rebellion, loss of vision and dreams, drugs or hanging out with the wrong crowd, their spirit (where the Spirit of the Lord helps them discern) goes to sleep. They do not respond to the Gospel or have dreams or visions. They do not look around and perceive that they are lost and asleep. They need God's forgiveness (Romans 10:14).

Pray that the slumbering spirit awake. Command it to awake! Command the plugs out of the ears. Command the blinders off the eyes. Command the soul (intellect, will and emotions) to respond to the Spirit of God (Ephesians 5:13-15).

DEATH

If people have not moved through a normal grieving process, cried, sensed the loss, experienced the anger or accepted and received the healing and assurance of God in death or loss, they can take on a great heaviness in their hearts.

As a young child, I was unaware of the grieving process. Not knowing what my future held, I could not let down my defenses and grieve for the breakup of my parents' marriage and the subsequent death of my mother. In my subconscious, I held onto that moment and never grew emotionally beyond it. As I grew older, I developed violent allergies.

One day, after many unsuccessful medical treatments, I was driving down the road and the Lord spoke to me. He revealed I had supressed my grief and heaviness and was holding on to my mother. I immediately confessed and asked forgiveness and prayed that I may be released from the grief that had followed my mother's death. A huge weight rolled off my chest.

As you begin praying for Inner Healing, ask the Holy Spirit to reveal specific areas for healing. Recall the event and ask Jesus to walk through it with you.

SELF PITY

Because of hurt, one can feel self-pity. Self-pity is a very destructive emotion that can lead to depression, illness, mental or physical breakdowns. Self-pity is a negative form of self-worship for the focus is entirely on self. Self-pity is an emotion that can be controlled. You can choose not to feel sorry for yourself.

Everyone experiences hurt. Focusing on hurt magnifies its effect. Pity holds on to the past. If you focus on the past, you are held back from fully owning the future.

The way to be free is to constistently forgive and at the same time, learn wisdom so that you do not keep repeating the same set of circumstances and same mistakes. Hurt from family members will have to be addressed each time it happens.

PRAYER FOR INNER HEALING
Jesus, I asked You to personally walk through _____, (this painful memory) with me. I forgive the following people _____. I release this memory to You to touch and heal my memories. I invite the light of Jesus to fill this emotional hole in my life.

HEALING OF THE SPIRIT

Healing in the spiritual area is obtained through taking back the legal rights the enemy has to occupy. It can come through confession of sin, repentance, breaking generational curses, removing curses people have put you under or spiritual warfare. It can include discernment (a gift of the Holy Spirit) or through prophetic action. More information concerning this type of prayer is in *The Power - Christian Primary III*.

SUICIDE

Some people in extreme, negative stress have thoughts of committing suicide. These are suggestions from an evil spirit.

Some actually threaten suicide or attempt suicide. This is a serious cry for help. They cannot perceive any way out of their circumstances. Teenagers are perhaps more susceptible because of the turbulent emotions of just being a teen.

Lack of hope can be generated from negative circumstances, loss of support (friends, family, illness) suggestions from movies, friends, drugs, dwelling in self-pity, depression and influences from evil spirits (evil spirits are perhaps the ultimate force behind all suicidal feelings). Suicide can run in families as a generational curse. The root is the Deaf and Dumb Spirit (see *The Power - Christian Primary III*).

Intense feelings often pass if a person is kept safe over several days. Suicide threats or attempts should always be taken seriously.

PRAYER FOR DELIVERANCE
I repent and ask forgiveness that this suicidual spirit has been allowed in my family. In the Name of Jesus I remove all legal rights for this spirit to to maintain its hold on my family. In the Name of Jesus I bind this strongman and command it to leave through the doorway it entered.

REVIEW

God is triune. In His Kingdom God speaks a triune language. Living God's Kingdom is learning and understanding His Kingdom principles and His law of Love so that your may live a full and balanced Kingdom experience. Within this text you have considered these trinities:

The Godhead
Father, Son and Holy Spirit

Your Relationship to God
Salvation, Baptism in Water and Baptism in the Holy Spirit.

The Three Kingdom Standards
Love, Faith and Hope

Kingdom Healing
Body, Soul and Spirit

It is interesting to note that Jesus began His ministry at the age of thirty, died on the Cross at the age of thirty-three, exactly at three p.m. and, rose again three days later.

GO FORTH AND LIVE THE KINGDOM

Through the prayers in this text you can expect to receive freedom and to actually see more light. Light is the symbol for life and blessing (footnotes Genesis 1:3, II Samuel 22:29). Jesus is the Light of the World- expect to gain more clarity, more light, more understanding.

For the moment our journey together into knowing God's Kingdom ends. However, your journey to truly know God and His Kingdom is only beginning. Let not your journey be one of just faithful obedience, but also a journey of the heart and of relationship. Live with great expectation, spontaneity and joy! Lend your ear to the Holy Spirit to be your daily guide and you will always find the path true and full of adventure. God truly rewards those who love Him with an outrageous love. You have seen God's Kingdom! You have seen the King! Lift up your eyes, for before you lies a vista of hope and friendship for all eternity.

May the grace of the Lord Jesus Christ, and the love of God and the fellowship of the Holy Spirit be with you (Corinthians 13:14).

SPIRITUAL STRENGTH TRAINING SERIES

The Kingdom - CHRISTIAN PRIMARY I $13.00

This book offers a comprehensive overview of God's Kingdom and practical suggestions on how to enter into Kingdom living. It includes basic Kingdom structure, practical applications of faith, love and hope, and concludes with a study on physical healing and healing for the soul. ISBN 0-9718325-0-1

The Kingdom - TEACHER'S MANUAL $31.00

A teacher's manual to teach the Bible study *The Kingdom*. Developed by a veteran teacher, this easy to use teacher's guide offers chapter-by-chapter study guides, 20 pages of ready to use, hands-on activities, and the compete text of *The Kingdom*. It also includes a treasure map and art front plates from the four Gospels. ISBN 0-9718325-3-6

The Kingdom Journal - THE REVOLUTION BEGINS $13.00

The Revolution Begins is a student handbook/workbook for participants in a study course of the book *The Kingdom*. It is the companion text to *The Kingdom Teacher's Manual* containing Journal sheets for dreams, visions and words from God and all the necessary handout materials from *The Kingdom Teacher's Manual,* along with various other work pages to impact the student in their Kingdom journey. ISBN 0-9718325-9-5

The Glory - CHRISTIAN PRIMARY II $13.00

Jesus is the Glory! He is the light of the world. Man was created to walk in the light of the Glory of God. Here in this Kingdom coloring book, *The Glory,* explore colors, numbers and the anointing of King, Priest and Prophet, using color as a visual aid.
Available, 2005 ISBN 0-9718325-1-X

The Power - CHRISTIAN PRIMARY III $13.00

The Holy Spirit is the Power - the gift from God the Father - the Teacher and Guide to all Truth! This text offers a practical study of how to enter into a relationship with the Holy Spirit and how to practice deliverance. Negative color charts reveal how evil spirits operate.
Available, 2005 ISBN 0-9718325-2-8

ORDER: SPIRITUAL STRENGTH TRAINING SERIES
By phone: (503) 791-1922 Evensong Publishing
Online: www.amazon.com or www.booksurge.com
When ordering on line use author's name and name of the Book

Evensong Publishing
"Changing the World one Heart at a Time"

Made in the USA
Columbia, SC
07 June 2018